. . . . . .

To help you in developing and updating
your charitable giving plan,
all worksheets and exercises in this book
are available FREE on-line.

If you would like to download electronic versions
of the worksheets and exercises,
please visit

www.josseybass.com/go/inspiredphilanthropy

Thank you,

Tracy Gary

Melissa Kohner

. . . . . .

INSPIRED
PHILANTHROPY

INSPIRED
PHILANTHROPY

YOUR STEP-BY-STEP GUIDE

TO CREATING A GIVING PLAN

Second Edition

■ ■ ■ ■ ■ ■ ■ ■ ■ ■ ■ ■ ■

TRACY GARY and MELISSA KOHNER

Foreword by Suze Orman

JOSSEY-BASS
A Wiley Imprint
www.josseybass.com

Published by Jossey-Bass
A Wiley Imprint
989 Market Street, San Francisco, CA 94103-1741   www.josseybass.com

Jossey-Bass books and products are available through most bookstores. To contact Jossey-Bass directly call our Customer Care Department within the U.S. at 800-956-7739, outside the U.S. at 317-572-3986, or fax 317-572-4002.

Jossey-Bass also publishes its books in a variety of electronic formats. Some content that appears in print may not be available in electronic books.

Library of Congress Cataloging-in-Publication Data

Gary, Tracy, date.
 Inspired philanthropy: your step-by-step guide to creating a giving plan / Tracy Gary and Melissa Kohner; foreword by Suze Orman.—2nd ed.
 p. cm.—(The Chardon Press series)
Includes bibliographical references and index.
 ISBN 0-7879-6410-7 (alk. paper)
1. Deferred giving—United States—Handbooks, manuals, etc. 2. Philanthropists—Charitable contributions—United States. I. Kohner, Melissa, date. II. Title. III. Series.
HV41.9.U5 G37 2002
361.7'4—dc21   2002008576

Printed in the United States of America
SECOND EDITION
PB Printing   10 9 8 7 6 5 4

THE CHARDON PRESS SERIES

Fundamental social change happens when people come together to organize, advocate, and create solutions to injustice. Chardon Press recognizes that communities working for social justice need tools to create and sustain healthy organizations. In an effort to support these organizations, Chardon Press produces materials on fundraising, community organizing, and organizational development. These resources are specifically designed to meet the needs of grassroots nonprofits—organizations that face the unique challenge of promoting change with limited staff, funding, and other resources. We at Chardon Press have adapted traditional techniques to the circumstances of grassroots nonprofits. Chardon Press and Jossey-Bass hope these works help people committed to social justice to build mission-driven organizations that are strong, financially secure, and effective.

Kim Klein, Series Editor

Contents

■ ■ ■

PART ONE

Creating Your Giving Plan

PART TWO

Strategic and Creative Ways to Leverage Your Giving

List of Figures, Tables, Worksheets, and Exercises

■ ■ ■

Figures

Tables

Worksheets

Exercises

Foreword

Suze Orman

■   ■   ■

When charitable requests come in the mail, making a pitch for your support to stop global warming, prevent cancer, fund a local food bank, or preserve a nature conservancy, do you read the letters? Throw them away with the supermarket circulars? Or do you give as much as you can?

There are scores of good causes, and many of us feel we can't afford to give to all—or any. The larger view suggests that we can't afford not to give to some. There's a moral component to the issue, of course, and everyone has to decide privately how much he or she owes the world. But there's another factor to consider, one that's not often mentioned. When you donate money to a cause you believe in, you're giving yourself the gift of power.

Familiar scene: You're sitting in front of a stack of monthly bills, writing checks and watching your balance shrink. You come upon an envelope from an organization that supports a charity you care about, or maybe a cause you've given to before, when you felt flusher, or a group whose work you've always admired. Hard-pressed this month, you toss the envelope away, gather up your paid bills, head for the mailbox and set out to run some errands. You feel depleted.

Let's play it another way. While writing checks, you discover an envelope you know contains a worthy plea and, instead of throwing it away, you open it, read the letter and write another check—for $25 or $100; the amount doesn't matter as long as it won't break the bank. As soon as you've signed your name, the light dawns: Hey, come to think of it, you can spare a little money this month. Later, when you head out to pick up the kids from their soccer game, you're lighter on your feet—having discovered new resources of both good fellowship and funds, you're a little less pressured. You're buoyant, proud. Confident, curious. Ready to give and receive. And that's when wealth of all kinds comes your way.

It's really this simple: By giving, you become the receiver of gifts—not the smallest of which is an acquaintance with your own power of choice and your freedom to exercise it for the good.

Preface

■   ■   ■

We are honored to collaborate with writer and editor Nancy Adess and publisher Jossey-Bass in this second edition of *Inspired Philanthropy.* Since the book first appeared in the fall of 1998, the world has changed. The September 11, 2001 attacks on the United States and their aftermath are forever in our collective conscience as a reminder that what we do every day—the nuances of our actions and the values they express—do matter. It is, in fact, the heart cracked open by people and conditions so like or different from ourselves that moves the soul to open wider the purse.

We believe that key to truly creating changes needed to make the world work fairly for more people will be changing the giving process and the practices of those who give. If philanthropy is to facilitate substantial change, serve humanity and the planet, and support social capitalism, then all of us—donors, novices and experts, new and old—must put more planning into our giving.

We first came to write this book as a tool to help make more order out of our own and others' intentional generosity. We had heard from so many donors that they loved to give but felt less effective than they wanted to be. Many said they knew that for the sake of humanity and improving the state of the world or their communities they "really should get more organized or focused" in their giving. We knew the feelings.

There are now more than 1.6 million nonprofits in the United States alone. It can be overwhelming to know where your donations will do the most good or have the most impact, especially if you want to be strategic or consider making substantive change to address the root causes of social inequity and global distress. It takes a great deal of experience, consciousness, research, and time to become a good donor.

We are both donor activists, having been raised by socially active parents, giving grandparents, and religious traditions that showed us how to extend grace and goodwill to others. We were told to "leave the world a better place," or to "do something for the city, country, and community" in which we lived. Our parents and those who came before them, along with our mentors, showed by their examples the amazing gifts received from being a giving person—that true abundance within comes from giving and being connected to community.

Religious congregations and circles everywhere are successful in raising money because the collection plate keeps coming around. There it is: you give. As Melissa wrote in the preface to the first edition:

> It was from that collection plate that I understood that this was how the church kept itself in this building. But for other nonprofits, we must be much more decisive. The appeals come in the mail—what do you want to support?
>
> Thinking ahead of time about what you're committed to and what you want to give to commits you to accomplishing a goal. Putting your values and mission and commitment on paper challenges you to be as serious about your giving as nonprofits are in needing your support. Most important, it holds you accountable to giving of yourself and your money.

We offer this expanded edition at a time when philanthropy and the nonprofit sector contribute to the soul of societies across the world. While business and government do their parts in a democracy, the nonprofit sector brings heart and hope to us all, over and over again. What kept us feeling a sense of possibility after September 11th were the outstanding extensions of generosity that helped to heal us: volunteerism soared and billions of new dollars were given by first-time donors all over the world as expressions of concern and commitment.

Philanthropy is becoming a tool for democratic decision making and effective community building. It is no longer acceptable for it to be merely an instrument of self-interest for the wealthy.

We have tried to present the stories as well as the techniques that have moved us to be better donors and leaders. While all of the stories in the book are true, some names and other identifying information have been changed to preserve privacy. Here from the preface to the first edition is part of Tracy's motivation:

> At the height of my giving I was receiving requests from more than 700 groups a year. Unlike my parents, who are very organized about their philanthropy, as a younger donor I was not so organized, and found myself bouncing around from project to project, reacting to whatever came along. I came to realize that there was not only a personal consequence to my disorganization, but that it also affected others when I couldn't find proposals sent to me, or wasn't sure if there was any logic to supporting one project over another. I needed to refine my methods.
>
> I had noticed that foundations had guidelines and statements of purpose or missions for their work. As a result, they knew what they wanted to fund year by year; groups seeking funding saved countless hours by knowing a foundation's priorities. Following their example, I began to put my own vision for my work into words, stating what my dreams were and what communities had taught me was needed, and refining them in a manner that could be shared.
>
> This process gave me added energy and the focus to find partners for my work.

Creating a giving plan and being proactive with it may not only change your life, it might change the world. We have seen the remarkable gap that exists between people's stated desires for societal change and their irregular practices at contributing to making that change. Consciously accepted responsibility for our own role and our collective roles in shaping the direction of our society is one solution to the distance between nonprofits' needs and donors' giving.

This book is dedicated to helping us all bridge that gap in order to affect the more compelling gap that calls us to action: the co-existence of the greatest wealth alongside the greatest suffering in our country and the world. We have seen that awareness of our participation as donors and thoughtful decision making—at every financial level—will help create a more compassionate world for ourselves and the planet.

As Adrienne Rich has written:

My heart is moved by all I cannot save:
So much has been destroyed.
I have to cast my lot with those
Who age after age, perversely,
With no extraordinary power,
Reconstitute the world.

Let us imagine anew our collective abilities to align our dreams, deeds, and dollars.
With gratitude to all who have inspired us,

May 2002

Tracy Gary
Ross, California

Melissa Kohner
Philadelphia, Pennsylvania

Acknowledgments

. . .

We join many people who teach and model strategic philanthropy and volunteerism. We offer this workbook in the spirit of all of our collective work. On the second edition, Elizabeth Share provided research and writing assistance on new models in philanthropy, David Perrin researched statistics and organizations in the field, Melanie Wagner obtained permissions for quotes and reprinted material, and Jessica Chao provided extensive feedback on content.

Nancy Adess's extraordinary editing, consistent energy, and good humor were indispensable to producing the first edition. Working with her again on the second edition has been a blessing and a trusted partnership.

A special thank you goes to Christopher Mogil and Anne Slepian for shaping and fine-tuning the exercises and to More than Money for additions to the Resource section. Joan Fischer and Cheryl Altinkemer also contributed exercises developed in their work with alumni associations. Paula Ross contributed graceful and creative editing and writing at a key point.

For allowing us to quote them or draw directly from their stories and inspiring work we thank Angeles Arrien, Harriet Barlow, Frank and Ruth Butler, Stephanie Clohesy, Ralph and Jean Davis, Barbara Dobkin, Marta Drury, Marvin and Kathleen Factor, Elizabeth Faulkner, Michal Feder, Sarah Feinberg, Greg Garvan, Dana Gillette, Sylvia Giustina, Alison Goldberg, Sally Gottesman, Matt Howe, Si Kahn, Andrea Kaminski, Peter Karoff, Peter Kent, Tatjana Loh, Tom Lowe,

Doug Malcolm, Tracey Minkin, Cate Muther, Margaret E. Olsen M.D., Suze Orman, Steve Paprocki, Joan Peterson, Michele Prichard, Adrienne Rich, Sarah Silber, Marilyn Stern, Eve Stern, Brad Swift, Chet Tchozewski, Miven Booth Trageser, Marion Weber, Mike and Janet Valder, Léonie Walker, and Wendy Volkman.

The following organizations allowed us to quote from their materials: AAFRC Trust for Philanthropy, Asian American Federation of New York, Changemakers Foundation, Chardon Press, Condé Nast, the Community Foundation for the Capital Region, Grantmakers Without Borders, Grants Management Associates, Grassroots Leadership, Haymarket People's Fund, Inequality.org, Independent Sector, Minnesota Council on Foundations, More than Money, the Morino Institute, Jewish Fund for Justice, Ma'yan, National Alliance for Choice in Giving, National Committee for Responsive Philanthropy, National Center for Family Philanthropy, National Network of Grantmakers, The Philanthropic Initiative, Transformative Philanthropy Project, United for a Fair Economy, and the Volunteer Bureau of America.

Thank you also to the Arden Theatre, Jenny Bernstein, Susan Beyrle, Frances Bowles, Ames Cushing, the members of the Donor Organizer's Network, Diane Foster, the Institute of Noetic Sciences, The Women's Philanthropy Institute, Laura Loescher, Leigh Morgan, Meehan Rasch, Andy Robinson, The Shefa Fund, Linda Welter, and Tori Williams.

We owe our gratitude to Kim Klein and Stephanie Roth of Chardon Press for bringing the first edition to print and for their important contributions to the world.

Thank you to Liberty Hill Foundation which, through its stewardship with donors, was a learning laboratory for this workbook. Resourceful Women, through its groundbreaking work with women donors and its extraordinary members, provided much of the initial background for this workbook.

T.G. and M.K.

About the Authors

Tracy Gary has been a donor activist and philanthropic advisor for more than twenty-five years. She supports and educates donors, family foundations, financial service organizations, and nonprofits in the stewardship of money, leadership, and philanthropy through Community Consulting Services, which she founded in 1978. She lives with her partner in Houston, Texas and the northern California bay area, collaborating on the Giving Institute. She has founded seventeen nonprofits, including Resourceful Women; the Women's Foundation of San Francisco; the International Donor Dialogue Network; The Women Donors Network; and her latest venture, the Changemakers Fund, for which she is currently raising $20 million to expand and strengthen community-based philanthropy. She has served on over thirty boards of directors and has been recognized nationally and globally as a force for justice and community building. She has traveled to build communities through philanthropy over one hundred days a year for the past twenty years and is available for keynotes, trainings, and workshop presentations for foundations, donors, nonprofits, and financial service companies (Web: www.massmanassociates.com). To provide feedback on this book, please send an e-mail or fax (tracygary1@aol.com or 713/528-9167).

© Audie England

Melissa Kohner is an organizer of young donors and leaders, building a young-donor movement to help transform philanthropy. She has worked nationally to address the political and financial concerns of donors of all ages through individual and group consultation and workshops. She has been a speaker at conferences and organizations ranging from the Council on Foundations to the Women's Funding Network and honored as an organizer. She has worked in community economic development, fundraising, and grantmaking and has served on numerous grantmaking committees. She is a board member of Lion Theatre and Bread and Roses Community Fund and serves on the steering committee of the Young Donor Organizing Alliance. She can be reached by e-mail at msk4@aol.com or by fax at 215/574-4951.

Introduction

∎ ∎ ∎

When you give money or time to a cause, does it speak directly to something you really care about? Do you feel confident that your money or time will make a difference, help improve the world? Do you feel sure it will be used wisely?

This book is for anyone who has a deep desire to be engaged in helping others and in making the world a better place. Even if you don't think of yourself as a "major donor" or a "philanthropist," this book is for you. Because if you've given away any amount of money—from a dollar to buy a raffle ticket for your local senior center or cultural center to thousands of dollars to a favorite charity—or volunteered any amount of time—from a few hours a year as an election polling place monitor to several hours each month on a crisis hotline, from serving meals in a church kitchen to serving on the board of a nonprofit organization—you are indeed a giver.

Like most givers, you may not have thought systematically about whether the resources you give reflect your own personal philosophy and priorities or even whether they are being used as effectively as possible. And, like many donors, you may be frustrated by the scattered way your giving takes place—responding to a mail appeal that strikes your interest, giving to a friend's favorite charity, to your religious congregation, to a college alma mater, the Red Cross, or going to a couple of benefit events each year. All of these gifts may be supporting important nonprofit activities, but none of them may feel directly related to what you are personally passionate about.

Helping you move from what we call "obligatory giving" to "inspired giving" is what this book is about (see Figure I.1). By the time you have worked through *Inspired Philanthropy,* you will be more familiar with the place of nonprofit organizations in the world, the values you want to see reflected in nonprofit work, and the impact you can have by joining with organizations that truly speak to your values. You will be closer to being a passionate giver—both effective and inspired.

Inspired Philanthropy has grown out of more than fourteen years of our experience working with people who give. We have consulted with the donors, staff, and boards of nonprofit organizations throughout the county; with members of national funding networks and donor education programs such as Resourceful Women, The Funding Exchange, Changemakers, Social Venture Network, Resource Generation and the Coalition for New Philanthropy; and with hundreds of individual givers. In this workbook, you'll find that we ask you to think about your deepest hopes for a just world, how to have impact in creating change, and where you can find your place in working for that world.

Creating a giving plan

Chances are you give some amount of money away. Whether your giving is substantial enough to justify itemization on your tax form or hovers around a thousand dollars a year, it is important that each dollar given and each hour spent have the greatest impact. Whether to give to the recipients of traditional philanthropy or to activities fostering social change is your choice. In either case, by following the thoughtful planning steps presented in this book, you'll succeed in maximizing the benefits of your gifts.

Inspired Philanthropy will lead you through the steps to align your giving with your dreams of a better world. Creating and using a giving plan will give you a sense of control, purpose, and direction and will inspire you to become more proactive in organizing, managing, and taking charge of your financial life in general. A thoughtfully developed and conscientiously implemented giving plan will tell

Figure I.1 The Inspired Philanthropy Paradigm.

American households, on average, give $1,075 per year to charity, spread among ten donations. Most of these gifts fall into the "obligatory" sphere. You can turn your current giving upside down with inspired philanthropy.

Becoming an inspired philanthropist

Here are two stories from people who became inspired givers.

Tracey Minkin

Our early giving was to the Sierra Club because my husband was a member. Every time they called we'd give $25 or $35, but we had no idea how much we were giving over a year's time. One day I came across a brochure about giving that said that the people who earn the least give the most and that everyone should give 5 percent of their income. I went right home and suggested to Jonathan that we begin doing that.

The following year we made a list of our donations and noticed that, aside from gifts to our colleges, almost all our giving went to environmental groups. Although we were interested in social services, the environmental groups were the ones that had reached us. So we created categories of where we wanted to make donations—education, arts, environment, social services, and a slush fund—and earmarked $2,000 (5 percent of our gross income of $40,000) to distribute.

As our income has risen so has our giving. We divide it according to percentages we agree on for each category of giving and among groups we research. And the slush fund serves for whatever comes up—friends who ask us to buy tickets for things, for example. Our donations range from $25 to $1,500.

Each January we have what we call the Budget Summit. We used to have a bottle of champagne and have a party, just the two of us—that was before we had kids. We review our previous year's giving and look at the groups in the slush fund to decide whether to include them in one of the other categories. We look at whether there will be anything big this year. For example, Jonathan wanted to give $1,000 to his 20th college reunion; next year he'll probably only give $250 and that will free up $750.

We keep track of our giving on a spreadsheet on the computer; with a few years all on one sheet, we can compare giving from previous years. We project how much the 5 percent is going to be and we go down the list to see what we did last year. We ask ourselves if we like the mix of groups. We talk substantially about how much to give to each group, trying to be realistic about the impact of the money. For example, $100 goes further at the local shelter than at a national environmental group like The Nature Conservancy, so we give a little more to The Nature Conservancy because we feel they're spending our money well. We're also interested in making a difference in our town, so we look for local opportunities to give.

We look at annual reports when they come, but not very closely. Instead, before the Budget Summit we have a lot of conversations on the fly about what we call good works. We've decided to put human or social services over other concerns, especially work for the well-being of children, and we value local over national or international efforts. By the end of the summit, we list all the groups we want to give to for the next year.

When we get solicitations on the phone I ask them to send information or, if they are on our list, I ask them to send a pledge card that I will use. It makes it easy to always have the same answer.

When fundraising letters come from the groups on our list I write a check and note it on the spreadsheet. The major national environmental groups and schools do a good job of finding us and asking for money. Some groups who are on our list never ask us. In December, I write checks to groups that haven't asked. If something comes up during the year—for example, if I see an ad for the Women's Center and it looks like they need the money right now—I'll send them a check.

Sometimes you have to swallow hard to do this. We made less money this year so it's tempting to say, we could use this money this year. But we so firmly believe in philanthropy that we rely on our plan to keep us committed to our program—giving should be that way. It's too easy just not to do it.

I think people should start giving in their 20s, when they have a lot of energy and optimism and creativity, so that it becomes a habit. It's also a time when you can get cynical if you're working at some low-paying job. Giving some money or volunteering is a great way to reaffirm your faith in the world and connect to something.

Miven Booth Trageser

My first giving plan was hopelessly ambitious and way too fragmented. I had been writing my will and decided that I wanted 60 percent of my assets to go to specific nonprofit organizations and 40 percent to specific individuals.

I noticed that the checks I had been writing as donations over the previous two years had gone primarily to groups working on women's rights, community organizing, and alternative media. I decided that each of these three areas would receive one-third of the 60 percent. I designated ten organizations within those areas and the proportion I wanted each of them to receive. When it came to naming individuals, ten people came to mind to whom $100 to $1,000 would make a difference and I named them in the will.

Making this plan forced me to realize that I can't give to everything. I had to confront that feeling of not being able to do enough for the world, that I have limitations.

Then I thought, if I'm planning my giving for when I'm dead, what's stopping me from doing it now? That's when I decided to use my will as a blueprint for a yearly giving plan.

After a couple of years of trying to give according to the plan, I realized it wasn't working out. The plan included too many groups, which meant I wasn't focussing my giving in a realistic way. I discovered that there were three organizations to which I'd given more than $250 each year for several years—Liberty Hill Foundation, the Labor Community Strategy Center, and Co-op America. It felt good to realize that these were three organizations I had a good relationship with and felt good giving to each year, and that I could simplify my giving plan by focusing on them, as they support a range of activities I care about.

I know that there are lots of organizations I'm ignoring. I can't even let myself read their literature because I feel too upset that I'm not going to give them anything because I'm committed to my plan. At the same time, there is something nice about saying no— I'm not going to spread myself any thinner.

I have never had a year where I followed my plan exactly the way I thought I would. I still find myself giving $30 to random phone solicitations or $10 at the front door. I thought the plan would arm me against that, because I would know I was being strategic. But I have a very hard time saying no to a kid at the front door.

you where your philanthropic hours and dollars are going and, because it reflects your personal priorities and dreams for creating a better world, it will be an active ally in supporting the issues that are most important to you.

Giving to individuals outside of the family—as opposed to charitable organizations—is, generally speaking, a norm in some communities and cultures and a strongly held value for many people across very different traditions. While we will not be directly addressing the process or nuances of making these gifts to individuals, the same principles of inspired philanthropy apply to these gifts as to gifts to organizations.

Our world is growing more complex; environmental degradation, world strife and enormous social needs make thoughtful attention an ever more pressing demand. The good news is that there are more resources and tools for addressing these issues. As a donor, you can choose to join the tremendous opportunities for collaborating with those who share your vision, for seeding new ventures, for breaking down racial and socioeconomic barriers. As a person who cares about what happens in this world, your effectiveness, creativity, leadership, and hope are needed as never before.

We offer *Inspired Philanthropy* in a shared spirit of partnership for societal change.

How to use this book

The book is divided into two sections. Part One will ground you in a context of the nonprofit sector and philanthropy, give you the chance to examine your own giving patterns, and help you identify the skills that you bring to the nonprofit sector. The exercises and examples in this part will guide you through the process of creating a mission statement for your giving and naming specific goals for the amounts of money and time you want to give.

Two chapters focus on where you want to give and provide ideas for researching, and developing your own giving plan, with plenty of examples for guidance. When you have finished Part One, you will have a road map for your giving and volunteering

Part Two provides useful information on how to work with nonprofits as a

Some beliefs about inspired philanthropy

- Everyone has a role in changing the inequities of society, regardless of income or class.

- Philanthropy is a creative expression of that part of yourself that cares about and believes in the potential for change.

- The most effective philanthropy joins your interests and experiences with the current needs in your community and seeks desired outcomes.

- Thoughtful, planned giving gives you a chance to express yourself and your passion as well as your goals and reasons for giving.

- Creating a giving plan fosters more enjoyment, ingenuity, and effectiveness in personal philanthropy than automatic, reactive giving.

- Coming into your own true place of giving is an evolving, definable, and developmental process.

- Inspired philanthropy and service have transforming powers for all—givers and receivers.

donor, what vehicles and strategies you might want to consider to direct your giving, ideas for sparking children and teenagers to give, and a chapter for donors giving $25,000 or more.

The appendixes contain a visual depiction of the Inspired Giving model, additional ideas on being an effective giver, a section on considering making loans to friends, sample letters, and an extensive resource section of useful materials, organizations, and other resources.

We recommend that you read the book through once, then go back and do the exercises, write your mission statement, and complete your giving plan. You may want to make copies of the exercises and start a folder or binder for them along with drafts of your mission statement and other materials so you can refer to them easily.

You might also want to consider working through the exercises with a group of friends or family members or consult a professional advisor in developing your individual giving plan. Groups around the globe are using this workbook, one chapter at a time, to become more intentional. Many readers have found that working with others both broadens one's perspective and maintains one's momentum toward becoming an inspired philanthropist.

INSPIRED PHILANTHROPY

PART ONE

Creating your giving plan

. . . .

Chapter 1

Giving and
the nonprofit world

■ ■ ■

Within six weeks of terrorists attacking the United States on September 11, 2001, more than $1 billion had been donated to support the bereft families of the approximately 3,000 victims of the attacks. Americans throughout the country poured forth their help: donating blood, sending food, traveling to New York City to help sort through the wreckage of the collapsed World Trade Center buildings, and counseling those who grieved and mourned. Within days, the nonprofit sector—the Red Cross, the United Way, community and private foundations—along with corporate America, set up ways for their constituents, clients, and staff to express their sorrow and despair through compassionate action and gifts to nonprofit organizations.

The nonprofit sector had never been more important as a means for expressing concern through generous giving by people from all walks of life.

Why give? Charity, social maintenance giving, and progressive philanthropy

People give for all kinds of reasons, from family tradition, a sense of obligation, or an expression of faith to a desire to act on passionately held beliefs. Most giving falls into the traditional or charity model of responding to acute, immediate crisis needs—blankets and food for flood victims, temporary housing for homeless families. The ability to respond to crises is one of traditional philanthropy's strongest assets. Traditional philanthropy is also very good at supporting the established institutions—educational, research, religious, social, and cultural—that maintain and improve mainstream society and its structures. Traditional philanthropy is based on responding to, treating, and managing the consequences of life in the social order as it has developed in our country.

Progressive philanthropy, on the other hand, analyzes and responds more to cause than effect. Progressive philanthropy supports what is called "social change"—that is, actions that seek to identify and address the root causes of disadvantage or practices that threaten values such as equity or a healthy planet. For example, once warm and dry, flood victims may want to join together to advocate for effective yet environmentally sound flood control methods, including relocating businesses and houses out of the flood zone. For homeless people, a sweat-equity program of home building and private-public partnerships for job training and education might provide more permanent solutions to their needs than shelters and food kitchens. While the need for mainstream, crisis-healing philanthropy remains, there is also a need to go beyond the Band-Aids to the wounds themselves and their source.

Progressive philanthropy strives to fund work that is pro-active rather than re-active, work that speaks to the underlying causes of people's distress. Progressive philanthropy's investment lies in challenging the assumptions that economic and social inequities are somehow unavoidable as the price of "progress" or "prosperity."

The public face of American giving

Since institutional philanthropy's beginnings with the wealth created by the industrial giants of the late nineteenth and early twentieth centuries, the dominant public face of philanthropy in the United States has reflected the concerns of society's powerful elite. As the scholar Lisa Durán points out in the *Grassroots Fundraising Journal,* "Definitions of philanthropy have been dominated by a view that emphasized 'charity,' the detachment of professionalism, the benefits of tax deduction, and giving through charitable institutions."

At the same time, as Durán notes, philanthropic giving has never been restricted to the wealthy elite. Even though they have not been included in the traditional definition of philanthropy, immigrant communities and communities of color in the United States have a long history of giving traditions and philanthropic institutions. *(Grassroots Fundraising Journal,* Vol. 20:4, 2001.)

New views of philanthropy allow for a conception of philanthropic behavior that includes nontraditional ways of giving, as well as the giving of time, shelter, or other material resources beyond the nuclear family. For many, giving to extended family and friends is an integral part of their philanthropic values.

Social changes of the last fifty years have also brought changes to the world of philanthropy. In the United States, social and economic justice movements dating from the Civil Rights Movement of the 1960s, and including the Student Movement of the 1970s, the Women's Movement of the 1970s and 1980s, and the Lesbian and Gay Civil Rights Movement of the 1980s and 1990s have helped to spread power beyond the wealthy elite, focusing on a more democratic decision-making structure. The changes in global communications wrought by widespread use of the Internet along with the growth of the world economy have expanded our definitions of community and mobility and brought more attention to the links between the causes and effects of our actions. These sea changes have also affected philanthropy and how it is defined. We are connected as never before.

One of the goals of the movement toward a more democratic form of philanthropy has been to shift the power to decide where philanthropic dollars go. Once these decisions were the sole purview of those giving the money; now, however, many foundations involve people from communities receiving funding as decision makers.

At the same time, some of those who were slated to take over the reins of traditional philanthropy have altered its course. Many who inherited wealth in the 1960s, 1970s, and 1980s wanted to develop alternative avenues for funding that would support groups seeking the more fundamental social change represented by the social justice activities of their time. Toward that end, they started a number of public foundations across the country that are now dedicated to addressing some of the root causes of inequity, including exploitation, racism, sexism, and homophobia, and to broadening the traditional view of who gives to support fairness in America.

Among other things, these foundations fund community organizing activities and sponsor alternative cultural institutions, including street theater, neighborhood arts, and activist media. The progressive funding movement that these inheritors began now includes networks of funders, such as the Funding Exchange, the National Network of Grantmakers, and the Women's Funding Network, and many associations of givers to specific issues or populations.

More recently, the expansion of the global economy and our increased ability to communicate and learn through the World Wide Web have prompted new efforts to broaden philanthropy's scope.

Nonprofits: An essential link

Nonprofit organizations are the most common vehicle in the United States for funneling money and other resources to areas of need. Nonprofits provide services, education, and advocacy in a multitude of areas—from arts and culture, education, health, and public safety, to religion, recreation, counseling, and community organizing. If you've ever checked out a library book, taught someone to read, helped an immigrant learn English, provided legal aid, made a donation to the American Cancer Society, contributed to your church or school, volunteered as a monitor for a gay pride parade, donated your used clothing to a battered women's shelter, bought Girl Scout cookies, attended the ballet or opera, taken an aerobics class at your local YWCA, donated to a scholarship fund or been a member of the Lions or Links Club, you've been a citizen of the nonprofit world.

Nonprofit organizations, sometimes collectively referred to as the independent sector, are legally incorporated organizations defined under section 501(c)(3) of the Federal Tax Code as exempt from corporate income taxes because of their mission to accomplish some charitable, humanitarian, or educational purpose. No owner, trustee, or stockholder shares in any profits or losses of nonprofits.

A statistical view shows the enormous contribution of the independent sector to the country's economy. According to the *New Nonprofit Almanac: Facts and Figures on the Independent Sector 2001,* in 1998 there were 1.6 million nonprofit institutions in the United States, including schools, hospitals, human service agencies, arts and cultural organizations, churches, synagogues, temples, and mosques. In the same year, the independent sector employed an estimated 10.9 million people, accounting for 6.1 percent of the national income and representing more than $700 billion in revenue. That year, 109 million people volunteered; the value of their time is estimated to be more than $225 billion. The nonprofit sector employs nearly 10 percent of the American workforce—more than all the federal and state governments combined.

It is clear from these facts that nonprofits of all types play a crucial role in the social, economic, religious, cultural and community aspects of our lives.

That's a lot of money

According to *Giving USA 2001*, the annual yearbook on American philanthropy, donations of non-governmental funds to nonprofits totaled $212.00 billion in 2001 (see Figure 1.1). This amount is an increase of 0.5 percent from 2000.

If you're like most people, you probably think that most of the funds that go to charitable causes come from corporations and foundations. You're in for a surprise. *Giving USA* shows that more than 82 percent of the money given away in 2001—and for many years before that—came from individual donors (including those whose giving came in the form of bequests, that is, gifts distributed after their death). Corporations contributed 4.3 percent of the total, and foundations 12.2 percent. This general pattern has held true for a number of years.

When most of us think of the philanthropy of individuals, we think of large gifts by very wealthy people to such nonprofit institutions as universities, hospitals, museums, and other traditional arts organizations such as symphony orchestras and ballet and opera companies. In 1997 Ted Turner's $1 billion gift to the United Nations, followed soon thereafter in 1999 by Bill Gates's $24 billion endowment to the Bill and Melinda Gates Foundation, set a very generous and even surreal standard.

The wealthy aren't alone in their giving, however. People who toil all their lives at low wages manage, through an irrepressible spirit of generosity, to be major donors

By Source of Contributions

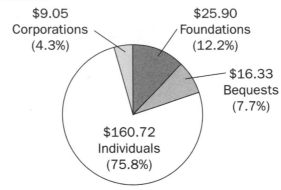

$9.05
Corporations
(4.3%)

$25.90
Foundations
(12.2%)

$16.33
Bequests
(7.7%)

$160.72
Individuals
(75.8%)

By Type of Recipient Organization

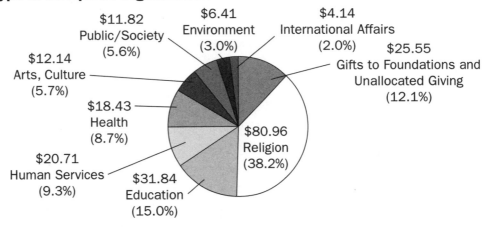

$11.82
Public/Society
(5.6%)

$6.41
Environment
(3.0%)

$4.14
International Affairs
(2.0%)

$25.55
Gifts to Foundations and
Unallocated Giving
(12.1%)

$12.14
Arts, Culture
(5.7%)

$18.43
Health
(8.7%)

$20.71
Human Services
(9.3%)

$31.84
Education
(15.0%)

$80.96
Religion
(38.2%)

Figure 1.1 Giving 2001: $212.00 Billion.

American Association of Fund Raising Counsel Trust for Philanthropy/*Giving USA 2001*

as well. Oseola McCarty spent a lifetime washing and ironing other people's clothes. In 1995, when she was 87, she had saved enough money to give $150,000 to the University of Southern Mississippi. Her donation established a scholarship fund to benefit African-American students. When honored for her donation, Ms. McCarty repeatedly expressed her wish to continue giving. Similarly, Thomas Cannon, a retired postal clerk, has given more than $96,000 in the form of $1,000 checks to individuals in need, although the most he ever earned was $32,000 a year. Many of his gifts go to strangers whose good works he reads about in the newspaper.

According to INDEPENDENT SECTOR's *Giving and Volunteering in the United States, 1999,* seventy percent of Americans contribute to charitable organizations. Perhaps most surprising, the bulk of money going to nonprofits actually comes from households with incomes of less than $60,000. Looked at another way, in 1998 contributing households with incomes of less than $10,000 give away an average of 5.3 percent of their household income to charity, while those with incomes of $100,000 or more give less as a percentage of income—only 2.2 percent. Contributing households with incomes between $40,000 and $50,000 give on average only 1.4 percent of their household income. In relation to income, then, our largest and most generous donors are those who are the poorest. Nearly 40 percent of all donations in America are given through religious institutions, which distribute humanitarian aid and other community services.

This means that whether you give a lot or a little, when you join the community of donors—to traditional philanthropy or social change—you join millions of other Americans who make charitable gifts and support nonprofit work that speaks to their ideas of caring and commitment to one another and the world.

The role of private philanthropy

While private support of nonprofits rises a little each year, over the last few decades government support of nonprofits has been diminishing. As impossible as it is for private individuals to completely offset the government's extensive budget cuts to social services and arts institutions, the role of the individual donor is nevertheless increasing in importance as more and more nonprofits lose their governmental financial underpinnings.

During the 1990s the country's economy boomed and, as Figure 1.2 shows, a small percentage of families at the top of the economic ladder became much wealthier, including through stock earnings in a long bullish market, while the income of families at the bottom did not keep pace.

Rising Together: Change in Family Income, 1947-79, by Quintile and Top 5%

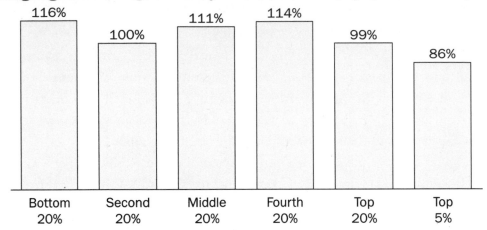

Drifting Apart: Change in Family Income, 1979-98, by Quintile and Top 5%

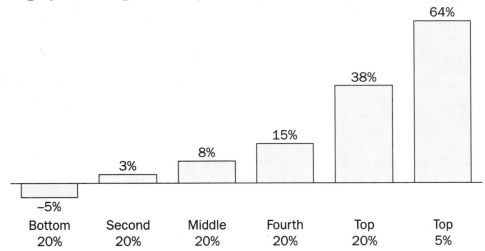

Figure 1.2 Income Inequality.

Sources: 1947-79: Analysis of U.S. Census Bureau data in Economic Policy Institute, *The State of Working America 1994-95* (M.E. Sharpe: 1994) p. 37. 1979-98: U.S. Bureau Historical Income Tables, Table F-3.

(Adapted from http://www.ufenet.org/research/income_charts.html)

How nonprofits affect our lives

■　　■　　　■　　　■　　　■　　　■　　　■　　　■　　　■　　　■　　　■　　　■　　　■

Nonprofit organizations express some of the most caring aspects of our humanity and our desires for equality and justice. More than we may realize, our world counts on volunteers and donors.

What if there were no nonprofit organizations? Imagine . . .

- No local churches, temples, synagogues, or mosques
- No low-cost tuition and financial aid at schools or colleges
- No cultural centers or community theaters, symphonies, or museums
- No zoos, community gardens, or farmers markets
- A victim of domestic violence or rape without counseling and legal defense
- A town without a volunteer fire department or local Girl and Boy Scout chapters
- No community organizations fighting for justice
- No social clubs, business associations, or service clubs
- A rural or inner-city community without a health clinic
- No AIDS, alternative health, or cancer research
- Lesbian, gay, and questioning youth without welcoming crisis phone lines
- Natural disasters without the Red Cross and international aid
- No homeless shelters or soup kitchens
- No services for immigrants or refugees
- No groups fighting to protect our environment and endangered species
- Injured or lost animals without humane rescue teams
- No food banks, Salvation Army, or Goodwill

What's underfunded

Nonprofits serve some of the greatest, and most marginalized, needs in society. This list gives an idea of the kinds of groups that need more funding.

- International groups
- Bilingual programs, products, and services
- Environmental groups
- Groups serving people of color
- Groups led by people of color
- Groups serving low-income women and girls
- Programs for refugees, migrant workers, and immigrants
- Groups serving lesbians, gays, bi-sexuals, and transgendered people
- Community-based arts programs
- Rurally based programs
- Inner-city programs
- Youth organizing
- Prison reform
- Alternative health care programs, prevention, or research
- Mental health services for low-income clients
- Programs for single parents and their families
- Low-income or affordable housing
- Programs and strategies to further systemic change
- Policy research and advocacy
- Collaborations, especially statewide or international
- Alternative media and access to media and technology
- Public interest law and legal aid
- General operating support (instead of project-specific funds)

Inspired philanthropy poses two important questions: Given the currently low levels of government funding for social services and other nonprofit activity, what is each person's responsibility to help? And do those with higher incomes or more assets have a greater responsibility?

We believe that everyone has a responsibility as citizens of the human community to give as much of ourselves as they can. After all, why do we have to accept such widening gaps between the rich and poor? Why in fact, should such degrees or conditions of poverty exist at all? For those of us whose personal wealth or earnings have grown over the years, we feel we should consider matching our expanded financial resources or longer-term asset growth with equally strong community generosity.

What motivates people to give

What is the inspiration that motivates people to give? The answer is, of course, somewhat different for everyone. Some follow the tradition and examples of giving and volunteering they were raised with. Others are moved by witnessing injustice or consider themselves moved by faith. What is almost indisputable is that in the act of giving time, skills, or money, we all feel the spark of our original inspiration, which propels us to continue giving.

The following are inspirational stories of donors with strong motivations and passions for giving and an organized, focused vision that has developed over time.

John Gage: Living and giving simply

A former monk, I left the Jesuit order ten years ago when I was 40, but I keep my vow of simplicity. I feel strongly that America is caught up in over-consuming, and I find it troubling that most people do not see or feel the effects of what I consider to be global greed. Although I live on less than $8,000 a year, I give away 6 percent of my income. I still focus my giving on the goal of "restoring right relationship between peoples and the planet" that informed the giving practices of my Jesuit order.

In choosing which nonprofit organizations to donate to, I create a giving plan that includes setting a budget and establishing annual mission statements—what I call "hopeful goals." To fulfill those goals, I follow a number of practices: I sort direct mail contribution requests regularly in order to help groups eliminate duplications and to keep informed through their updates, I support investigative reporting in order to learn more about who is working for social justice, I favor low-profile groups that don't send elaborate or multiple mailings and whose communications are environmentally sensitive, and I initiate personal contact with at least half of the groups to which I give in order to ask them what they need in terms of money or support.

Greg Garvan: Giving back

In the early 1990s I received an inheritance that gave my family many new choices. It also presented us with a number of questions: Do we give all or part away? Do we keep it for retirement? Save some for the kids?

First we followed the age-old advice not to make any major changes for a year. During the year we met with a financial planner to review our options. At the end of the year, we had made our decision: we would give 25 percent away outright and with the rest set up gifts to nonprofits through a vehicle called charitable annuities (see Chapter Ten) that would add income to our retirement funds.

I decided I wanted to support small groups that others might not be funding and that would have some personal meaning to me. Since my family had owned a textile company for 120 years in the South, the profits of which had contributed to my inheritance, my wife and I decided to give back to those people whose relatives had been underpaid by the textile business.

Through my own travel and research I found small organizations not funded by larger regional foundations that help local minority farmers and new businesses. One was the South Carolina Farming Association's Seeds of Hope project, which links black farmers with local churches to set up farmers' markets. The program had become so successful that churches far outside the local area wanted produce for their own farmers' markets. To be able to transport fresh produce to these more distant markets, the project needed a refrigeration truck. Learning of this need, my family and I provided the money to buy the truck.

In another philanthropic area, I convinced my siblings to join me in supporting the Black Historical Society and in honoring a black woman who had helped raise us by establishing the Carrie Kilgore Scholarship at the College of Charleston. This was a modest way of saying our thanks to someone who gave so much to each of us. My family and I also helped the Institute of Southern Studies, publishers of the magazine *Southern Exposure,* with a year's start-up funding to hire a marketing and fundraising specialist.

My advice to donors is to talk to folks. Groups usually know what they need or want to try. Do you have the ability to respond to their request? Try to do some homework about the group's financial situation or vision, or check out their collaborations. Have fun doing it. If you're lucky enough, a good part of your community nonprofit investments will work and be a spiritual experience. In the meantime, you'll also grow and learn so much about your community. What could be better!

Peter and Jonathan: A couple's commitment

We are both committed environmentalists and give regularly to nonprofits. When we read that the Women's Forest Sanctuary in California needed investors to help refinance mortgages on their fourteen acres of old-growth redwoods, we decided to help. We sold some of our stock and loaned the money to the Forest Sanctuary for a modest 6 percent return. Though this meant a lower return than we had been making in the stock market in those days, the decision was gratifying. It gave us the chance to feel part of saving one of the world's greatest resources. As a side benefit, we eliminated the higher capital gains taxes we had been paying on those high-earning stocks.

Given that we're only in our 30s, have good earning potential, and don't need to use income from our stocks now, this was an easy decision—but our love of the trees was the highest value.

Chapter 2

You, the philanthropist

■ ■ ■

For most people, philanthropy is not an occupation—it is an offshoot of whatever they do with the rest of their time. Even if philanthropy occupies a larger share of time, to think of being a philanthropist can raise a multitude of negative stereotypes and assumptions. We all carry stereotypes of philanthropists, though we may not be conscious of them most of the time. Allowing ourselves to recognize these stereotypes and then contrast them with our actual experience helps to free us from long-held biases and reconsider identifying as a philanthropist. Check out your own ideas about philanthropy in Exercise 2.1.

Let's look at this notion of philanthropy a little more closely. The word *philanthropy*, derived from Greek, literally means "love of humankind." According to the *Oxford English Dictionary,* a philanthropist is "one who from love of his fellow men exerts himself for their well-being; engages in practical benevolence towards men in general." Inspired philanthropy expands that description to define as philanthropists "all people who exert themselves for the well-being of others; who engage in practical and heartfelt benevolence; who donate money and time to causes they believe in so that the world may become a better place."

If you've given away money (or volunteered time) you're a philanthropist, whether you donate millions to a new hospital wing, a few hundred dollars to a community health clinic, or $25 to a nursery school raffle. The money can come from earned income, inherited wealth, or a windfall at a bingo game. The two

Stereotypes

10–20 minutes

Allow yourself to write whatever comes to your mind, uncensored. By getting at the ideas that are just below the surface we can begin to identify our stereotypes—and, if appropriate, discard them.

Typical philanthropists:

(Example: Are from old money; are older than 55; live in mansions)

a. _____

b. _____

c. _____

People I know who give are:

a. _____

b. _____

c. _____

As a giver I am:

a. _____

b. _____

c. _____

Reflection: What have you learned about yourself by doing this exercise? For example, you may have found that your stereotypes contradict your experience or that the terms "philanthropist" and "giver" elicit different reactions.

_____

_____

_____

_____

essential ingredients are *giving* and *caring*. When you give to things you care deeply about, your philanthropy develops special meaning.

There is no threshold of activity one must do or money one must give to qualify as a philanthropist. Philanthropy is the design and manifestation of your hopes, dreams, and wishes. If you don't do so already, calling any donations of time or money your "philanthropy" will give it the intention it deserves. You give because you care about others.

Creating a giving plan is a process of distilling what you love and are concerned with, and threading those issues with your own values, money, and time. Creating a giving plan means choosing initiatives, leaders, and nonprofits whose missions and strategies are working to make the changes you want to see. Here is one Oregon philanthropist's description of her giving.

Sylvia M. Giustina

For the last ten years I have been giving monthly checks for charity. I started out giving $10 per month, and now I give $15. At Christmas time I give more. I give 2 to 3 percent of my total take-home income. I give away in five checks a month. I give to a domestic violence shelter called Raphael House, the Oregon Food Bank, the Red Cross, Northwest Medical Teams, Dogs for the Deaf, the Anne Frank Center, Oregon Heat, and the Brady Center to Prevent Gun Violence. I also tip really well. Once a year I give to the Brady Campaign to Prevent Gun Violence, which is the Brady Center to Prevent Gun Violence's lobbying arm; that gift is not tax deductible. Several of these charities are also in my will.

For Raphael House I also buy music CDs and CD players and batteries. I go to Circuit City where they have a lot of discount collections. I like giving music because it's something I enjoy. The people at Raphael House love it when I drop off music.

I don't have a family of my own and I like to shop and buy stuff at Christmas time. I found a bookstore that sells remaindered books for $1 each. So one year I spent about $50 dollars there on books and brought them to Raphael House.

I decided I also wanted to give gifts for teenagers. After the incidents at Columbine High School I realized how vulnerable a lot of teenagers are. I bought some music and books for teenagers and I gave them to the Salvation Army. A fire-fighters' charity called Toy 'n Joy collects things at Christmas for kids, and they said they were having a hard time finding stuff for preteen girls. I did some research and found some really good books for that group. Books are not that expensive. I look for stuff that's quasi-educational, including the *Diary of Anne Frank* and also blank books.

One of my favorite gifts is ice cream. I give gift certificates to Baskin Robbins. I mail them to people when I read about things in the newspaper.

You only have so much control and so you do what you can in small ways. I know that I work better with concrete things than with abstracts. I've connected my head and my heart. I really love books and music and food. I don't think my gifts of music and CD players are changing people's lives but they are lifting someone's soul.

What do you care about?

Philanthropist Harriet Barlow describes the feeling she gets from giving this way: "Giving well requires that I listen to my inner self and make more conscious who I am and what I want to express in the world. That's why giving is almost always satisfying to me—whether or not the projects I fund are successful."

Mary Lam, on the other hand, discusses whether Chinese people rely too much on feeling in their giving: "We Chinese give, but it's only from the heart. We need to use a little more mind behind our giving. Of course, coming from the heart is important. This is where it starts—a sense of gratitude, or a feeling of obligation to those we care about or who gave to us. But then we really need to find ways to extend our financial gifts and make them work for us with more impact."

Knowing what you feel passionate about is the first step in determining where your personal contributions of money, time, and energy will feel most effective. Your financial resources are part of who you are. Giving money and time is about giving a part of yourself. The next exercises ask you to look at what you value most and whether your funding choices to this point reflect those values. For many philanthropists, giving is not only a way to express their values, it also helps them articulate what those values are.

Exercises 2.2 and 2.3 will help you clarify your values as a giver.

Our values are characteristics we hold in high esteem, what we give worth to. We may value qualities of being, such as integrity and justice, or particular kinds of endeavors, such as working for justice for the oppressed, feeding those who are hungry, or elevating the status of women. Whether we are conscious of them or not, our values greatly influence our behavior as givers, including what we fund, how we evaluate projects, and how we relate to those we support. For example, if you value women's leadership, you may make it a priority to fund programs that give women opportunities to develop leadership skills. Even if a program you're interested in is not specifically oriented to women, you may want to know what percentage of their members and key staff are women.

What do you bring with you?

Working with organizations is, for many, an unexpected source of satisfaction. Experienced donors report that some of the benefits of their work have been developing and sharing a wide variety of skills. Putting what you do well in the service of a cause you feel passionate about and being recognized for your contribution feels wonderful. In turn, you'll invariably learn more, which is another reward.

In the last exercise, you explored what's important to you and what you believe in. Now use Exercise 2.4 to give some thought to the skills, knowledge, training, and background you have to offer. These may be personal experience with an issue area, specific expertise and knowledge, or other skills and abilities you can put to use.

Here is how another philanthropist pulls together her values, beliefs, and life journey.

Sally Gottesman: Changemaking

Here is the truth: I am discontent with the world the way it is. This is a funny thing to write—I feel so lucky to be alive, to feel the heat from the sun falling on my arm, to look at the flowers sitting on my desk. I have the ability to read, to write, to breathe, to be filled with awe and humility for feeling at one with the Universe in the here and now. And yet, I am discontent. I want there to be peace. I want God to be called in *my* image, in Hebrew and in English (and all languages). I want the birth of Jewish girls to be celebrated with equal communal joy as the birth of Jewish boys. I want all children to have food to eat tonight, and every night.

I am a changemaker because I want the world to be a better place for everyone. I am a changemaker because I have identified those issues about which I am most passionate, and I get pleasure from working on them and giving to them. I am a changemaker because I have found partners in my endeavors. And I am a changemaker because I recognize that I can use my brain, my time, and my money to indeed make the world a better place.

Two adages guide my efforts and give me energy as an activist and donor. The first is by Margaret Mead: "Never doubt that a small group of committed people can change the world, indeed it is the only thing that ever has." And the second is from the Talmud: "You are not required to complete the task nor are you free to desist from it."

I choose to concentrate the majority of my efforts for change, in terms of both financial resources and volunteer time, on a variety of organizations. I am inspired by the work of these organizations. I feel a passion for their missions, and to the core of my being, I believe they will help shape a world that is a better place for women and men, girls and boys.

I am blessed to have been raised in a family that values volunteerism and philanthropy. Early impressions guide me: my grandfather's stories of raising money for Palestine in the 1920s on the New York subway, my grandmother making me a life member of Hadassah; with my sisters, organizing a carnival in our back yard to raise money for multiple sclerosis when I was ten. Finally, there was the experience of my advocating for and becoming the first Saturday morning bat-mitzvah at my family's Conservative synagogue. All these experiences imbued within me a sense of personal responsibility and proof that I could make a difference.

Indicators of Your Values

15–20 minutes

In whatever way works best for you—free writing, quiet thought, or a conversation with a friend—explore one or more of the following questions that you find interesting. Write your answers below.

- What experiences and people have been key in shaping your core values and passions?

_____

_____

_____

_____

- What do you notice about your values when you consider your choices, such as life directions, career, free time, lifestyle, donations, and spending?

_____

_____

_____

_____

- When you hear of world events or witness an injustice, what moves you most? With what have you been most troubled? Most delighted?

_____

_____

_____

_____

_____

_____

What I Value

15–25 minutes

Listed here are words or phrases that express values. Feel free to add any that are especially meaningful to you.

Values

Acceptance	Faith	Love
Access	Family	Opportunity
Beauty	Freedom	Peace
Commitment	Generosity	Preservation
Communication	Harmony	Respect
Community	Healing	Responsibility
Compassion	Honesty	Service
Courage	Honored Obligations	Simplicity
Creativity	Innovation	Stability
Democracy	Interdependence	Transformation
Dignity	Integrity	_____
Diversity	Justice	_____
Equality	Joy	_____
Empathy	Knowledge	_____
Excellence	Leadership	_____

Choose from this list your top five values. Now, even though it may be difficult, out of those five choose your top three and record them here.

Top three values:

1. _____

2. _____

3. _____

On the next page are words or phrases that describe issue areas and populations that you may care about as a contributor. The areas provided are only for inspiration. You may never have donated time or money to these areas of interest before; this exercise is simply to give you the chance to recognize what has meaning for you among things you could give to.

Issue Areas and Concerns

Ageism

Animals and Species
  Preservation

Anti-Semitism

Anti-Racism

Arts & Art Institutions

Biodiversity

Boys

Business Development

Catholic Charities

Children/Child Care

Civil Rights

Co-existence

Community Gardens

Computer Literacy

Corporate Responsibility

Cultural Heritage

Death and Dying

Demilitarization

Disability Rights

Disaster Relief

Drug & Alcohol Abuse

Domestic Violence

Economic Justice

Education

Elder Care

Employment Training & Job
  Creation

Environment/Environmental
  Justice

Electoral Reform

Faith-Based Community Service

Gay/Lesbian/Bisexual/
  Transgendered Civil Rights

Girls

Gun Control

Healthcare & Prevention

HIV & AIDS

Homelessness/Housing

Homophobia

Human Rights

Immigrant & Refugee Rights
  and Services

International Development

Jewish Causes

Legal Aid & Legal Services

Libraries

Literacy

Media

Medical Research

Islamic Causes

Native & Indigenous Peoples'
  Rights

Nutrition and Hygiene

Parks & Land Preservation

Peace/Conflict Resolution

Philanthropy & Volunteerism

Poverty

Prison Reform

Public Policy/Advocacy

Religion

Reproductive Rights

Science & Technology

Seniors

Spiritual Development

Sports & Recreation

Sustainable Development

Women's Rights

Youth Development

_____

_____

_____

_____

_____

_____

Choose from this list your top five areas, then your top three. List these here. If one of the three is of absolutely the highest priority, star it.

Top three issue areas and concerns:

1. _____

2. _____

3. _____

Reflection: Do you see a relationship between your top values and your top interest areas? Here are two examples:

1. My top three values are dignity, equality and opportunity and my top three issue areas are education, economic justice and youth development. I believe that the opportunity for a good education, particularly for young people who are shut out of their full potential early on because of poor schools, is vital to dignity, equality and, finally, economic justice for everyone.

2. My top three values are community, justice and respect and my top three issue areas are seniors, poverty and homelessness/housing. The relationship I see is that in order for everyone to live in a just community, all seniors must have enough financial support, including good housing, to lead their lives with respect.

Write down the relationships you see among your own values and interests:

_____

_____

_____

_____

_____

_____

_____

_____

_____

_____

_____

_____

_____

_____

_____

_____

_____

Time, Talents, and Treasures

15–25 minutes

What time, talents, and treasures do you bring to your passion? In the list below put a check mark next to each characteristic or item that is true for you. These may stimulate you to think of specific ways you want to share your abilities, which is the purpose of the second part of the exercise.

___ I can donate my professional skills to a nonprofit

___ My workplace has equipment or services or meeting space, I could offer to a nonprofit for their use

___ I'm good at organizing details and creating plans

___ I'm good at motivating people

___ I'm good at planning events and giving parties

___ I know many people in my community who might be good resources

___ I like to teach what I know

___ I am a good listener or writer

___ I have experience designing or administering Web sites

___ I am a supportive person to work with

___ I'm good with financial information

___ I like to raise money

___ I can translate or know people who can translate documents into other languages

___ I have graphic skills or artistic talents

___ I love kids or am good with elders

___ I am a passionate public speaker

___ I have ___ hours of time per week, or would be willing to take a day or more each month, to donate

___ Other:

_____

_____

Now look back at the top three values and issue areas you wrote down in Exercise 2.3. Think about the time, talent, and resources unique to you and your community that you can offer in working on those issue areas. For example, if you're a breast cancer survivor and one of your issue areas is breast cancer, you might write, "I have been through diagnoses and treatment and could help others know what to expect or just provide support." Or, if you're passionate about electoral reform and belong to a civic group or business roundtable, you could invite a speaker on the topic to make a presentation.

Write a statement of how you can offer your time, talents, and treasures here:

_____

_____

_____

_____

_____

_____

_____

_____

_____

_____

_____

_____

_____

_____

_____

_____

_____

_____

_____

_____

_____

_____

Chapter 3

Your current system of giving

■ ■ ■

Everyone has a system of giving. It may be as unsophisticated as the time-honored shoe box: throw every direct mail piece into a box and once a month, once a year, pull them out and write checks for the ones that appeal to you. Or it may be more spontaneous: write a check whenever an appeal strikes you as worthwhile, or someone asks, or an event seems like it might be important or fun. Or it may be as formal as directing your banker to send a check each November 15 to the charity your family has been supporting for generations.

Taking the time to pull together how you've been doing your giving and looking at it as a whole will tell you more about yourself than you may realize. To develop intention and consciousness about how you want to give—to whom, how much, when, and for how long—use Exercise 3.1 to look at how you've been doing it up to now.

Imagining a better world

The information you generated in the last exercise describes your present giving practices and something about how you operate as a giver. When looked at as a whole in this way, your giving choices may surprise you—both in showing where

Analysis of Current Giving

15–20 minutes

A. Recent Giving—To get a sense of where your giving has gone in the last year, fill out the chart below.

Organizations donated to in the last 12 months	Amount given	Why I gave

B. Characteristics of the Groups You Give to—Beginning with the list of organizations you generated, map your top ten groups on the chart below (see the list of strategies groups may employ following this exercise). Once you've done so, you'll begin to see the patterns of your giving.

Organization	Issues It Addresses (refer to list in Chapter 2)	Strategies It Employs (refer to the list that follows)	Size by Budget Small: Less than $250,000 Medium: $250,000– $1,000,000 Large: More than $1 Million	Age Start Up: 0–2 years New: 2–5 Years Established: 5–10 Years Sustained: 10 Plus Years	Scope Local, State/Regional, National, International

Reflection:

1. Within each set of characteristics, was your giving focused on certain categories, or varied? Were these intentional choices? If they were, what reasons were behind your choices?

_____

_____

_____

_____

_____

_____

2. What do you see as the pros and cons of the pattern your giving has taken within each category? (For instance, your dollars may have great impact on small, start-up organizations, but start-ups sometimes fail. Giving locally offers you personal connection, yet many serious problems are international in scope, and your dollar often goes further overseas.)

_____

_____

_____

_____

_____

3. Looking at the characteristics of the groups you've funded, is there anything different you would like to do next year? What? Why?

_____

_____

_____

_____

_____

_____

C. Your Relationship with Groups You Gave to

Look again at the groups you listed in Section B of this exercise, and take stock of the relationships you have with them.

1. With what number of organizations are you a
   ___ Recipient of the organization's services
   ___ Volunteer
   ___ Member
   ___ Board member
   ___ Staff member
   ___ Other:

2. With how many do you
   ___ Know people in the organization
   ___ Know people who have been affected or helped personally by the organization (or ones like it)
   ___ Know other donors

3. With how many did you find out about them through
   ___ Direct mail
   ___ Family, friends, social club, association, or work colleagues
   ___ Local public foundation
   ___ Media
   ___ Other:

4. With how many do you
   ___ Want your donation to be completely anonymous
   ___ Want your donation held in confidence (only one or two people in the recipient organization know)
   ___ Don't care whether your donation is known
   ___ Want people in the community to know you made a donation

5. With how many did you stay informed by
   ___ Reading newsletters or annual reports
   ___ Attending events
   ___ Meeting one-on-one with staff or board
   ___ Other: _____

   _____

Strategies for change

- Advocacy
- Capacity Building
- Coalition Building
- Demonstrating, Direct Action, or Public Education
- Economic Development
- Education, Training, and Resource Development
- Fundraising or Leveraging Funds
- Electoral Politics (Supporting Candidates and Initiatives; Voter Education and Registration)
- Grassroots Community Organizing
- Human or Direct Services
- Influencing Public Policy
- Mediation
- Prayer, Meditation and Reflection-Based Action
- Problem Analysis and Research
- Public Interest Law

For an analysis of commonly used strategies for change and what is involved in funding them, see Chapter Seven.

your priorities have been and in what characterizes the groups you have given to. The strategy, size, age, and scope of those groups reflect how they make an impact. Maybe it's time to take a new look at where you want to be part of creating change.

Exercises 3.2 and 3.3 offer you the chance to step back from the giving you've been doing and reflect on social change in a broader sense. They speak to the following questions:

- What are the causes behind the problems that concern you?

- What do you wish were different, and what might help change the situation?

Though these questions probably aren't unfamiliar, it's good to keep integrating new considerations and refining strategies. Realistic answers to these questions are usually complex, yet it is worth trying to articulate answers, even at the risk of oversimplifying, because you will learn a lot about what you want to be giving to. If Exercise 3.2 seems daunting to you at first, you might want to skip to Exercise 3.3 for another way of getting at your vision of what you might create. Whichever exercise you choose, keep in mind that, like most of the exercises in this book, this is not one you can do once and learn all you need to know. In fact, it may spark you to begin talking with others about why change is needed on issues you care deeply about, what changes could be most useful, and how you can contribute.

Pulling it all together

Here's your chance to play Monopoly for the public good. Instead of hoarding your money and buying up all the properties, use Exercise 3.3 to create your vision of how you would give the money away.

How social change happens

Exercises 3.2 and 3.3 may stimulate you to want to know more about what really causes things to change. Organizing, mobilizing people, and making change shift harmful practices toward more constructive behaviors. A lot of innovative theory has been published about social change, and moving case studies of specific issue areas exist as written documents, films, plays, and visual art (see Appendix F, Resources).

In the next week, take some time to locate some resources on an aspect of societal change that you would like to see happen. For example, look in a library or bookstore for books on the topic; look into a history or sociology class at an adult education center or local community college; list one or more people you could interview who have been effective at making change in an area you care about; watch a video or film on the topic; think of others you could talk to who have focused on an area that concerns you. You might interview a leader, another donor, or a staff person at a foundation that is making the kind of difference you hope to. Part of your job training and responsibility as a giver is to stay curious about what it takes to make positive change.

When you've laid out some options for what you want to look into and how, choose one or two of them and schedule time to do them in the next month or two.

Increasing your knowledge and experience will greatly increase your effectiveness as a citizen and a donor, and will help you refine your philanthropic mission. The next chapter brings together what you've learned about yourself and giving so far and takes you to the first step of creating your giving plan: your philanthropic mission statement.

Imagining a Better World

Part 1: 30 minutes/Part 2: 30 minutes

This exercise is in two parts—one cerebral, the other imaginative. The first part asks you and a support-ive, interested friend or friends to think deeply about an issue, how things came to be the way they are, and what might help create positive change. The second part calls on your imagination to move beyond the rational thought process to an imagined state of an improved world. The two parts do not have to be done together. An example of doing this exercise using the topic of homelessness is on the next page.

Choose one topic that is of significant concern to you—something you'd really like to have an effect on in the world. (If you're having trouble defining a topic, refer to the list of issues in Chapter Two.)

Part 1: How did things get the way they are?

What might help them to change?

With your friend who shares your interest or concern, brainstorm what you know about this issue and present some of your main questions. You may want to consider the effects of key historical events, public education and opinion, and the interests of proponents and opponents of various actions that could address the issue. This part of the exercise may lead you to do some research to inform yourself more fully about the issue. When you've completed your thinking, list some of the ways the issue has been dealt with in the past and possible ways to address it in the future. On the next page is an exam-ple using the topic of homelessness.

Part 2: Imagining a better world

In some quiet time alone, or with your companion of Part 1, project your imagination into a world in which the issue you discussed in Part 1 has been positively changed 100 percent. For example, imag-ine an end to discrimination, or all endangered species flourishing. Daydream about the specific circum-stances that would be different in this new world. Consider your vision for a just society.

When you're finished, reflect on your vision the way you would if you were thinking about a dream you had just woken from. Choose one piece that strikes you. Look for what is most exciting, intriguing or surprising in your vision, something you would love to see in your eyes-open, real-life world. Brainstorm with yourself or your friend ways this piece could inspire a new area to fund or a new approach to your giving.

An Example of Imagining a Better World

Topic: Homelessness

Part 1: Why is there homelessness in the United States? What might help this to change?

Key historical events, public opinion and interests

- Federal policies in the early 1980s sent a majority of patients in state institutions to the streets, and failed to provide the community services promised to help them

- Other federal cutbacks in the 1980s and 1990s have severely reduced funding for subsidized housing

- Many cities have instituted "panhandler" laws prohibiting homeless people from asking for money

- Widespread corporate downsizing and relocation to other countries beginning in the 1980s left many low-wage workers without jobs

- After many years of widespread, visible homelessness, the general public has become hardened to it and concerned about their own safety

- Many city governments seem more concerned about keeping homeless people out of downtown areas where they disrupt commerce than with trying to meet these people's needs for food and shelter

Questions

- What is forcing people to become homeless right now?

- How has the welfare reform legislation of the 1990s had an impact on homelessness? On immigration and homelessness? On migration and homelessness? On the increases in the prison population?

- What are the characteristics of different populations of homeless people (women with children, substance abusers, and so on)?

- What are the specific needs in my city? For example, are there enough shelters? Do they stay open year-round?

- What helps people to find homes and jobs again?

- Can philanthropy help find a good, long term solution to the gap between the homeless and those who are not homeless?

Possible actions and keys to change

- Proactive and humane government policies
- Job training for jobs that are actually available
- Subsidized housing programs
- Public education that emphasizes how close many families are to homelessness
- Expanded and improved government assistance systems that provide minimum financial security, basic health care, and mental health services, especially for families in distress
- "Living wage" campaigns, affordable housing campaigns, small business loans, and tax reform—all of which would contribute toward a more equitable distribution of wealth

Part 2: Imagining an end to homelessness. What characteristics would our culture have in order to eliminate homelessness?

Our culture would place a high value on everyone's quality of life. Nonprofit organizations, religious institutions, and city governments would support the infrastructure that provides services such as job training, career counseling, and apprenticeships. There would be enough safe, clean shelters for people who needed them, including adequate facilities for women with children. People who lost their jobs or suddenly had their income threatened for some other reason, such as family illness, would have access to friendly and forthcoming government welfare programs, including housing, food and transportation vouchers, and health care.

How to begin to help

One piece that might strike you is the need for job training and career counseling programs available to anyone who needed them. You could begin by phoning your local church, synagogue, homeless shelter, or city hall to find out what programs exist. You could then contact some of the programs to find out what they need most. They may need volunteers to help job-seekers go through the newspaper's classified section and phone employers, or they may need interview clothes and voicemail services for people looking for jobs, or bus and taxi vouchers for people going to interviews. You might see a way that you personally could begin to make a difference in the lives of some of the homeless people in your area.

Million-Dollar Visioning

30–45 minutes

1. From the list of values and issues you care about, choose one problem in society you would like to help resolve:

_____

_____

2. Now, imagine you have just been given $1,000,000 to give away or invest in solving that problem, with no strings attached. What would you do, who would you convene or hire to support your efforts, what institutional partners would you choose?

_____

_____

_____

3. What outcomes would you hope for in what time frame?

_____

_____

4. How would you be involved to maximize impact?

_____

_____

5. How would you share your vision with others?

_____

_____

6. What is holding you back from starting some of this work, even without $1,000,000 or more currently in hand?

_____

_____

_____

Chapter 4

Creating a mission statement

. . .

In the last chapters you looked at your stereotypes about what a philanthropist is; your values, interests and priorities; what skills you bring to the nonprofit world; where you've invested charitable donations in the past; and how you think the issues you care most deeply about might be changed for the better. All of this information will be useful in the next step: creating a philanthropic mission statement. Your mission statement should be a brief answer to the question, "What do I want to do with my giving and my time, and why?" Once created and refined to your satisfaction, your mission statement will guide you in developing your Inspired Philanthropy Giving Plan in Chapter Seven. If your family is giving together, now is the time to articulate a collective vision.

Writing your mission statement

The most effective mission statements are usually no more than two or three sentences—something you can easily remember and others can easily understand. Though a mission statement is brief, it needs to pack a lot of information, so it will take some work to get it to say just what you want.

To begin, review your top values and interests from Exercise 2.3 (Chapter Two). Next, revisit what you felt you could offer of your time, talents, and treasures in Exercise 2.4 (Chapter Two). Finally, look at where you imagined you might like to make some significant changes in the world in Exercises 3.2 and/or 3.3 (Chapter Three). With this information, you're ready to use Exercise 4.1 to try your hand at drafting a mission statement. The following examples provide some mission statements others have written. In them, the mission statement is in italics, followed by some of the action steps the writer is taking to make progress on their mission.

Your Mission Statement

25 minutes

Write your own philanthropic mission statement here. It should include 1) reference to your passionate interests, 2) what you think can help improve or change issues you care most about, and 3) what you are doing to support improvement or change (some action steps). We've provided room for a couple of first drafts.

First Draft:

_____

_____

_____

_____

_____

Second Draft:

_____

_____

_____

_____

_____

Final Statement:

_____

_____

_____

_____

_____

Some inspired mission statements from individuals and family foundations

1. *I seek to reduce the amount of violence within families in my community.* I do this by supporting family violence prevention programs, volunteering ten hours a month on parent telephone hotlines that seek to reduce stress in families, continuing my ten-year commitment as a Big Brother, and advocating for laws that punish crimes of violence against families and that protect victims of violence.

2. *I want to see social justice, economic redistribution, and racial harmony.* Therefore, I work for, donate to, and volunteer with organizations that involve ordinary people in confronting and changing the institutions and public policies that affect their lives. I especially like to support those organizations in which I am personally involved, or where I know leaders of the organization.

3. *I want to help immigrants to this country.* Everyone in my family from my grandparents' generation were immigrants and the country has been good for us. I fund groups that give immediate support to immigrants and help them obtain good free or low-cost legal aid.

4. *The Compassionate Soul Fund exists to model gift giving and to raise consciousness about women's multiple contributions to the world.* We fund feminist projects for social change and human rights, especially those that serve and are headed by indigenous women and women of color.

5. *The Seed Fund exists to provide seeds to low-income communities for gardening and soup kitchens.* We are a group of organic farmers who believe that healthy food and hands-on growing and cooking of food can change the health and well-being of any community. We make contributions of money and/or seeds to schools and projects that distribute seeds, and we establish community gardens and teach sustainable gardening.

6. *I believe that camp should be an experience available to all kids.* I've seen children gain enormous self-confidence, skills, and new friends through

camp experiences that have helped transform their lives. Our family has established the Campers Fund to give scholarships to low-income and disabled children who have never been to camp before. It is our family goal to help two to four kids per year with $500 to $750 each for scholarships to the summer camp of their choice.

7. ***The two areas in my life that I have a strong passion for are music and work against racism.*** I serve on the board of a local music program that provides music training both for inner-city kids who cannot afford lessons and for schools and communities whose music programs have been cut. I am using my professional knowledge on the finance committee and I'm managing the endowment fund. I give monthly to this organization, which will also receive a bequest through my will.

8. ***I seek to reduce the effects of industrial pollution on the environment.*** I believe that grassroots action by communities to oppose pollution in their neighborhoods is one effective way to address this issue. Therefore, I donate to nonprofit groups that confront this issue at the local level.

9. ***As a couple that has lived in this region for some time, we believe in supporting this community and its sustained economic and cultural development.*** Through our donor-advised fund at the local community foundation, we make multi-year grants to groups that provide job training programs and micro-enterprise loans to individuals.

10. ***I believe that nothing can positively affect a person's life more than a good education.*** Therefore I devote whatever extra money and time I have to helping students get access to the best educational opportunities available.

11. ***Our family's goal is to bring creative expression to our community.*** We fund art and photography classes for inner-city and rural young people, and have established a summer community arts program that works with more than 200 young people in our town each summer. In addition, we buy art from emerging artists for personal investment and joy.

12. *We aim to link youth around the world and enable them to collaborate on social change projects.* We do this though the development of a Web site, online chat rooms with multi-lingual translation, and periodic in-person convenings.

13. *Our family believes in libraries and literacy as a means of strengthening community.* We contribute to libraries and reading programs, especially those that are bi-lingual and that bring the community together.

Chapter 5

Deciding how much to give

■   ■   ■

The tradition of expressing compassion through giving and service is present in all religions and cultures and celebrated as acts of benevolence and means to bring peace, justice, and a sense of prosperity among people. Giving of your time and money is more than simply doing good. It is a conscious, intentional act to weave oneself into a caring culture.

Giving part of your income or assets, whether it is easy to do or a financial stretch, and giving a portion of your time out of a desire to share and help, are gifts that extend not only to the recipient but back to the giver as well. We believe that those of us who do not give, or who do not give at our real capacity, are missing out on a joyful, wise, and heartfelt experience. Moreover, if society is to reflect the real pluralism that exists around us, it is absolutely critical that we share our good fortune through compassionate action. In this chapter we explore some of your beliefs about your ability to give and the philosophy of different giving practices. The giving practices offer values-based approaches that may help you decide how much you want to give of your financial resources.

How much money do you think you have?

People's attitudes toward their personal resources of money and time are formed early. The level of financial safety and income your family did or did not have as well as messages you received while you were growing up about how to use money and time become both conscious and not-so-conscious beliefs and attitudes when you are grown. The socioeconomic class in which you were raised, the class backgrounds of your parents and extended families, and the class that you would currently describe yourself as falling within all exert enormous influences on how you think about money.

For example, if you grew up in a household where there wasn't always enough money for essentials like food and clothing, you may still be anxious about having enough food and clothing, regardless of how much income you have now. If your parents volunteered in religious activities or community programs, you may be more comfortable with the idea of donating time to a cause than someone whose background didn't provide such a model.

One way to reduce anxiety around money is to unearth the beliefs you hold about it. Do you feel, for example, that you have more or less than your share (see Exercise 5.1), or that you may not have enough in the future? Do you believe that you can or do earn enough money to support yourself and any dependents who may need your help? Your answers to these questions may provide helpful perspective on your anxiety.

Major giving practices

Another way to address your feelings about how much you have and how much you want to give is to articulate your values and beliefs about living compassionately in the world. Some of us were raised with or now follow a religious tradition that clearly spells out the role of giving money and time within a set of spiritual values or practices.

Here we describe the major practices of giving, some spiritually based, some not. Use them to help you develop or refine your own giving practices. Then use Exercise 5.2 to determine how much you want to give.

How Much Money Do You Really Have?

5 minutes

Most of us have a distorted idea of where we fall on the nation's economic scale. Check out your relative financial situation (based on numbers from the 2000 Census) in the following short quiz.

My household pretax income is . . . (check one)

____ less than $25,000 (29.3 percent of the population)

____ $25,000–$34,999 (13.3 percent of the population)

____ $35,000–$49,999 (16.4 percent of the population)

____ $50,000–$74,999 (20.1 percent of the population)

____ $75,000–$99,999 (11.0 percent of the population)

____ $100,000 or more (8.7 percent of the population)

____ $119,540 or more (4.6 percent of the population)

____ income in excess of $330,000 annually and net worth of $2.5 to $3 million (top 1 percent of the population)

No matter what your income, according to the United States Census Bureau, if you earn any money at all, you have more money than one billion people in the world. Worldwide, average annual per capita income is $800. ("Income Distribution to $250,000 or More for Households: 2000." Current Population Survey, U.S. Census Bureau, Table HINC-07. November, 2001.)

Knowing the above, do you feel you could be or would like to be more generous?

_____

_____

_____

_____

_____

_____

How Much Should You Give?

5 minutes

On average, Americans give away only about 2 percent of their income to charity. As mentioned in the Introduction, however, we know that many people give significantly more than that.

In thinking about what percentage of income you want to give away, you might start by looking at the chart below. Find your income level, and then look across the row until you see an amount that feels comfortable to you as an amount to give away. Look at the top of the chart to see what percentage that is. Do both the amount and the percentage feel right to you? If not, where is the disparity? If you have given in the past, what percentage of your income does your past giving represent? How does it compare with the amount or percentage you chose on the chart?

If your income is	and you want to give 2%	3%	5%	10%	15%	20%
$30,000	600	900	1,500	3,000	4,500	6,000
$40,000	800	1,200	2,000	4,000	6,000	8,000
$50,000	1,000	1,500	2,500	5,000	7,500	10,000
$60,000	1,200	1,800	3,000	6,000	9,000	12,000
$75,000	1,500	2,250	3,750	7,500	11,250	15,000
$100,000	2,000	3,000	5,000	10,000	15,000	20,000
$150,000	3,000	4,500	7,500	15,000	22,500	30,000
$200,000	4,000	6,000	10,000	20,000	30,000	40,000
$250,000	5,000	7,500	12,500	25,000	37,000	50,000

Note: You may choose your level of giving based on your pretax or post-tax figures.

This year I/we want to give $_____, which represents _____ percent of my/our income.

Next year I/we want to give $_____, which represents _____ percent of my/our income.

Stewardship

Many people believe they are merely shepherds of the money they earn or inherit and have a responsibility to use their money for the public good. This philosophy is based on the belief that claiming ownership of wealth reinforces the unequal power structures that enable just a few people to accumulate large amounts of money. Some who subscribe to this philosophy keep only enough money to cover their basic living expenses and give the remainder away. Notably, a number of people who inherited large amounts of money have given away all but enough to live an average, comfortable life. For some inspired reading about these donors, see *We Gave Away a Fortune* by Christopher Mogil and Anne Slepian (see Appendix F, Resources).

Tithing

Long held as a practice in many religions, tithing means giving away 10 percent of your income (a tithe is literally one-tenth). This practice is based on the belief that only 90 percent of what you earn (or inherit) actually belongs to you and the rest must be used for the good of humanity. This is similar to the notion of stewardship, but with a specific formula for guidance. Many people like the idea of basing their giving on a percentage of their income, but choose less (or, in some cases, more) than 10 percent as their benchmark. In Judaism, the notion of tithing is expressed as *tzedakah*, Hebrew for "righteous giving." In Islam, this same practice is called *zakat*. As in other religions, 10 percent is expected from all.

Workplace giving

Many donors participate in workplace giving campaigns whereby charitable donations are deducted regularly from employees' paychecks. The system is most often administered by a federation of agencies that are the recipients of the donation. Contributions can be made to a general pool or designated for specific member organizations or for particular issue or interest areas. The United Way has had the largest and best-known workplace fundraising appeal. Its funding focuses primarily on human service needs. Recently, community-based workplace funds have entered this arena. These new funds are not only building good track records but are also raising money at a rate higher than the United Way. There is a more extensive discussion of these funds and federations in Chapter Ten.

Many donors embrace workplace giving as a method of fulfilling their desires to give a percentage of their income without having to call on the discipline of making individual contributions from home. Other donors see their payroll deductions as a small piece of their entire giving plan. Also, because donations are spread out over the year's payroll periods and come from money the employee never actually has in hand, many use this method to give a sizable amount over the course of a year.

Giving away principal

Although not a giving philosophy per se, "never touch principal" has been such a time-honored belief among people with inherited or earned wealth that it deserves a mention here. In addition to the people mentioned above who have given away most of their assets, others who have inherited or earned wealth are choosing to give a portion of their assets during their lifetime. These assets can include stocks, bonds, real estate, insurance policies, and works of art. Given the intricacies of tax benefits for gifts of cash, appreciated assets, and planned gifts, if you are thinking of giving assets you might want to work with a financial planner or estate or tax professional to consider just how much is possible or advantageous for you to give. Here's how philanthropist Abigail Osinski considered the issue of giving away principal:

> I am considering a change in the way I handle my annual giving. I have always heeded the advice of my father to conserve principal whenever possible and spend only income. My income from investments has remained static over the years, but the value of the principal has ballooned. If I decided to give away a small percentage of principal annually, say 1 to 4 percent, I would be able to increase the amount of my giving tenfold at least. My investment advisors tell me I would be better off with this strategy than taking a portion of my portfolio and investing for extra income to give away.

Some facts on net worth in the U.S.

- Americans with incomes of $14,768 or less (the bottom 20 percent) have, on average, assets of –$7,075 (they are, on average, $7,075 in debt), whereas the top twenty percent (making $68,015 or more) have, on average, assets of $871,463.[*]
- Those with the top 20 percent of assets control 83.4 percent of the wealth in the United States.[**]
- The wealthiest 1 percent of Americans have more wealth (38.1 percent of the total wealth) than the bottom 90 percent combined (29.1 percent of the total wealth).[**]

[*]Michael E Davern and Patricia J. Fisher, Household Net Worth and Asset Ownership, 1995," Household Economic Studies, 2001.
[**]Edward N. Wolf, "Recent Trends in Wealth Ownership, 1983-1998," Table 2. Jerome Levy Economics Institute, April 2000. www.levy.org/docs/wrkpap/papers/300.html.

Tax-deductibility

Here are a few things to consider about the benefits of charitable giving to your tax situation:

- If you itemize on your tax returns, you can include donations to nonprofits of $250 or more. Get a receipt for your tax records with your name as donor, the date of the gift, and the amount given.
- Some volunteering expenses may be tax-deductible. Check with a tax advisor regarding out-of-pocket and travel expenses and what receipts are required.
- Gifts of appreciated stock, property, and cash have various beneficial tax advantages; check with a tax advisor.
- No one will benefit more from your IRAs upon your death than a nonprofit (due to taxes on money received by individuals upon someone's death). Consider listing your favorite groups as beneficiaries of this part of your estate at least.

Thinking a little bigger

Imagine a 28-year-old who gave $3,000 each year until she died at age ninety-one. In sixty-three years of lifetime giving, she would have given $189,000, not including any gifts that came from her estate after she died. Use Exercise 5.3 to calculate your potential lifetime giving.

How Much Will You Give During Your Lifetime?

5 minutes

Think for a moment of how much money you gave to nonprofits last year or, if you prefer, start with the figure you decided to give in Exercise 5.2. Now multiply that amount by the number of years you expect to live (for example, if your life expectancy is 88 and you are 48 now, multiply your giving by 40 years). Add to that an estimate of how much you've given away in your life before now. To the total lifetime giving that results, add an estimated value of the percentage of your assets (for example, 10–50 percent) that you will direct to be given to nonprofits you care about after your death.

$\qquad$ $ \underline{\hspace{6cm}}$ $\times$ $\underline{\hspace{6cm}}$
Your average annual giving   Life expectancy years from now

$+$ $ \underline{\hspace{6cm}}$ $=$ $ \underline{\hspace{6cm}}$
Total amount you have given   Total lifetime giving
up to now

$+$ $ \underline{\hspace{6cm}}$
Estimated value of a percentage of
your assets gifted upon your death

$=$ $ \underline{\hspace{6cm}}$

Chapter 6

Volunteering and skill sharing

▪ ▪ ▪

The tradition of volunteerism has a long history in this country. The organizations engaged in the work of making the world a better place almost always need people's time as much as their money. We give of ourselves in many ways: we give our time, our skills, our creativity, our ideas, and our contacts in order to uplift, and at times, to save others.

We all know how precious time is but we're often unhappy with where our time goes. Think about whether you're satisfied with the way you spend your time. Does it accurately reflect your values? Consider where you currently put your twenty-four hours a day, perhaps by thinking back over the last few days or weeks. Are there adjustments you'd like to make to align your passions with the amount of time you devote to them? Would volunteering some time remind you of what you have to contribute or help you connect with your larger world?

In this chapter you'll find statements from two people who volunteer, along with an assessment of skills you have to offer and want to acquire, an exercise to reflect on your current volunteer time, and some guidance on what to expect and what's expected of you as a volunteer. We also provide support and inspiration about volunteer leadership roles.

Time is also a resource

Volunteering your time on behalf of a cause or group you believe in can be just as valuable and rewarding as writing a check. It can also be very healing. After tragedies such as the terrorist attacks and natural disasters, many parents and children found that giving back helped them feel better. And while volunteering is not a substitute for the cash nonprofits need to keep the lights on and the rent paid, it's another way of giving and full of its own rewards.

If you've never been a volunteer, you may find it hard to believe that spending a few hours a week or month can make any real difference. But call your local volunteer center and ask them. Talk to friends, colleagues or family members who have volunteered. (Most Americans volunteer an average of three and one-third hours a week.) What you'll almost certainly discover is that volunteers tend to be hopeful people, full of faith and creative expression about their lives and the future of their communities.

Whether you're donating your time and skills to a small or large nonprofit, your participation in and support of the nonprofit sector makes a vital contribution to society. If you choose to involve more than just your money, you'll find a world that offers opportunities for skill building, social involvement, and deep satisfaction. Here are two examples of people who have volunteered.

Margaret E. Olsen M.D.: Giving back

My mother was a nurse and my father was born poor but became successful. They both believed in helping the next person; I carry that on. I'm a dermatologist and mother of two. Aside from my private medical practice, I volunteer about twenty hours a month for the profession. In fact, I find that my volunteer position—teaching beginning medical students how to approach patients, deal with ethical dilemmas and personality conflicts, and not to be intimidating—is really my most significant work. I get the students at the very beginning, so I have the chance to personalize medicine, give it a human face. I complain every time I go, thinking I'm not appreciated, and every time I come back enriched.

I also give talks for the American Cancer Society about skin cancer to Rotary Clubs and lifeguards and help at marathons doing skin cancer screenings for over-exposure to the sun. My position as Chief of Dermatology at the hospital is a volunteer position, and I also serve on volunteer committees there to hash out problems the hospital is having.

I have been on the advisory committee of the Dermatology Foundation Leaders Society to help with fundraising for research grants. My job was to ask fellow dermatologists and corporations not only to donate $1,000 to $25,000 each but also to ask ten more people to do the same. It is easy to ask someone to donate cash when I've done it myself. The Dermatology Foundation gives us fundraising training.

I am a firm believer that you can do everything, but not at the same time; you have to choose. I believe it's easier to give money than time. Anybody can give money; it takes a little more soul to give time. I do it because I want people to have a better quality of life, to be less fearful of their own medical problems, less fearful of the doctor–patient experience. I want all these people to pass that on, to have responsibility to help the next person.

Oscar L. Tang

Adapted from *A New Heritage of Giving: Philanthropy in Asian America*. New York: Asian American Federation of New York, 2001.

Displaced from China by war and revolution, I came to this country as a youth knowing I could not return to my homeland. America took me in, provided me with the opportunity to learn, and I became a citizen under the 1953 Refugee Relief Act. When I arrived here with no English, the schools I attended allowed me to catch up and develop a sense of my own potential. These American institutions nurtured fledgling family and Chinese values and taught me to adapt them to my new country. Central to my American experience was the focus on any individual's role in the larger community.

My late wife also came to this country under similar circumstances. In later years, we often marveled at the spirit that extended these remarkable opportunities to us at a critical time when we had little to give in return. This created in me a deep sense of obligation. I came to realize that selflessness is what gives our lives meaning beyond our own indulgence. The United States has a vast network of private voluntary institutions in countless fields where untold numbers of people give of themselves. Together this army of contributors renders this country unique and helps make it a richer, more open, more just society. We all benefit from their efforts.

So too, we must invest in sustaining this effort for others into the future. For me, what could be more appropriate than to return part of the fruits of my labor to the system that invested in me? Each time I participate in some worthy volunteer effort, I am re-energized and my gifts give increased meaning to my own achievement.

Use Exercises 6.1 and 6.2 in this chapter to focus in on what you want to offer—and learn—through volunteering, and where you might want to donate some of your time.

What volunteering in the nonprofit world offers

- A place where beginners can feel useful and that welcomes a range of skills, including simple elbow-grease
- An appreciation of diversity
- A learning environment with explicit social values and a commitment to expressing them
- A place to experiment with program, product, and services, where outcomes, not profit, are the motivators
- Opportunities to meet people with shared values
- A culture that integrates passion, creativity and practical needs
- Structures that may challenge and question traditional hierarchy and systems of power
- The satisfaction of seeing donations of money and time create change
- A place where skilled volunteers have influence
- A culture in which to enhance empathy and increase a spirit of generosity

Giving and Learning Through Volunteering

5–10 minutes

In 1998, 109 million people—55 percent of Americans—volunteered in nonprofit organizations. The value of their time was estimated at $225 billion dollars. Getting involved in any role, from stuffing envelopes to chairing board meetings, not only increases your connection to a particular organization, it often increases your understanding of the nonprofit world and your joy in giving.

If you would like to volunteer, a key step is assessing what skills you have to offer and what you would like learn. In Chapter Two you thought about what talents you could offer nonprofits. Below is a more detailed list of skills often valued. Since volunteering offers opportunities to learn as well as to give, use this exercise to define skills you would like to acquire as well as those you can share.

Put a check mark in the box after each skill in one of the three columns. This list will be helpful in finding a volunteer position in which you're both well-used and challenged.

	Good at it	Want to learn	Not interested
Verbal communication			
Conflict resolution	____	____	____
Giving effective feedback	____	____	____
Listening and interviewing skills	____	____	____
Office work			
Answering phones or making calls	____	____	____
Using computers	____	____	____
Designing Web sites and updating Internet access	____	____	____
Finances			
Bookkeeping	____	____	____
Planning and reviewing budgets	____	____	____
Preparing useful financial reports	____	____	____

	Good at it	Want to learn	Not interested
Fundraising			
Hosting a house party or other event	_____	_____	_____
Researching grant sources	_____	_____	_____
Writing grant proposals	_____	_____	_____
Writing copy for press releases or reports	_____	_____	_____
Asking individuals for money	_____	_____	_____
Organizational development			
Designing organizational policies	_____	_____	_____
Program planning and development			
Public relations and marketing	_____	_____	_____
Volunteer leadership	_____	_____	_____
Facilitating meetings	_____	_____	_____
Public speaking	_____	_____	_____
Training/teaching others a skill	_____	_____	_____
Graphic design	_____	_____	_____
Other:			
_____	_____	_____	_____
_____	_____	_____	_____
_____	_____	_____	_____
_____	_____	_____	_____
_____	_____	_____	_____
_____	_____	_____	_____

Analysis of Current Volunteering

10–15 minutes

In the chart below, list each group to which you donated time in the last twelve months, how much time you gave, what you did to assist the group, and why you chose to volunteer for that particular group.

Organizations volunteered with in the last 12 months	Number of hours	What I did	Why I volunteered with this group

Total Hours Donated: _____

Average per Week: _____

Reflection:

1. What is the relationship between your giving and your volunteering? Do you volunteer for groups that address your priority issue areas? Why or why not?

   _____

   _____

   _____

2. How do you feel about the balance between what you give and what you receive from volunteering? Do you feel your time and skills are used well? Are you getting the satisfaction or other rewards you hoped for?

   _____

   _____

   _____

3. If you could design your volunteering to have the greatest impact on issues you care about it, how might it change?

   _____

   _____

   _____

4. If you could design your volunteering to bring you the greatest personal satisfaction, how might it change?

   _____

   _____

   _____

5. What is your next step in finding rewarding volunteer work?

   _____

   _____

   _____

   _____

Creating families with a culture of service

In some families, habits of giving, service, and volunteering are encouraged from a very young age. In others, kids learn about community service only because they are required to perform a certain number of hours of it to graduate from high school.

Imagine if, instead of going off in many directions each Saturday or Sunday, families were to do even three hours of service or community action together: building a house with Habitat for Humanity, working to educate the public on an upcoming voter issue, or creating an opportunity for a family to take a step out of poverty. These good deeds enhance our compassion, our skills, and our faith in our families as units of good will.

Volunteering for leadership

There are now more than 1.6 million nonprofit organizations in the United States with an expanding need for donors, volunteers, and leadership. The model of taking a step from donor to "donor partner" suggests one way to offer your leadership skills to organizations you fund. It comes from Changemakers, a foundation that promotes community-based philanthropy.

A donor partner uses her or his skills and contacts on behalf of a nonprofit organization as a supplement to giving financial support. Donor partners might step into positions of leadership as advocates, as members of grant and fundraising committees, or by engaging in special projects, while simultaneously being an ally to staff and community members. Through a formal and deliberate process, the donor and the organization draw up an agreement about the most helpful advocacy and action steps the donor partner could take to work with the nonprofit. The following are keys to a successful *donor partner*–organization relationship:

- Mutual accountability and formal or informal contract between the donor partner and the organization.

- Prioritizing the evaluation component of the donor partner's work.

- Active listening on both sides and an ongoing feedback loop.

Ten ways to be a good donor partner

1. Make a significant donation to the organization representing the level of your care and respect.

2. Keep up-to-date with the activities and accomplishments of the organization so that you can be a stronger advocate for their work.

3. Make clear to the organization that you want to be a partner and work with the leadership to define what that would mean, ensuring some form of accountability and feedback as part of an agreement.

4. Ask the organization's leaders what is needed.

5. Offer to help with things you're comfortable doing.

6. Offer to stretch to do something you're less comfortable doing, building in ways of getting support along the way.

7. Ask your friends and colleagues to support the organization.

8. Host an event and invite your contacts, or write personal fundraising letters to people you know who might have a value connection with the organization.

9. Accompany the executive director or development staff on a fundraising visit.

10. Help the organization get specific feedback about its effectiveness in program delivery and fundraising from donors and others in the community.

If you take on some specific tasks with an organization, use the questions in Worksheet 6.1 to clarify what's expected from you and what you want the organization to know about your work style.

Joining in the Work

Use the questions here to clarify your role and agreements with an organization whose work you will be joining.

1. What is my job description?

_____

_____

    Is my position one of staff (paid or unpaid), volunteer leadership, or intern?

    _____

    _____

    Have I been given authority to make decisions? What kind?

    _____

    _____

    How long will I be in this position?

    _____

    _____

2. To whom am I accountable and how?

_____

_____

_____

    What are my expectations for reporting and advancing the work?

    _____

    _____

How are others to be accountable to me?

_____

_____

3. How will I get the work done?

_____

_____

How will I build relationships and learn how the organization works?

_____

_____

4. How will I let others know how I work best (for example with communication, by phone or mail, best times to reach me)?

_____

_____

5. What training or orientation do I need or is being offered and is it adequate?

_____

_____

6. What background reading can I do and what questions do I have?

_____

_____

7. Are there meetings I could attend as an observer in order to support my orientation?

_____

_____

Using your skills as a nonprofit board member

Another way to be a volunteer leader is to join one or two boards of directors of your favorite organizations. Here are some ways you can be most productive on nonprofit boards:

- Only choose a board that you can be passionate about to others. Ask for a job description before joining a board and be sure you can meet the requests, including the financial and time commitment expectations. Read the bylaws; ask for the organization's most recent budget and financial report. Ask also about the health of the relationships between board and staff.

- Be sure you get a proper orientation to the board. If there is no formal mentorship or orientation process, ask for a guide or buddy to coach you on the board and the organization's history as well as any process issues you may need to know about.

- Be punctual for meetings and try not to miss more than one meeting each year. If you must miss a meeting, be sure to let your board president and the staff know ahead of time.

- Ask how you can be of greatest help and offer your skills, time, and talent as you know them. Be an ambassador or evangelist for your organization. Engage others in your passion for its work.

- The best skills you can bring are your listening and your full presence. This means reading the minutes and all the information regarding the organization *before*, not during, the meeting. (Consider making your own list of what you think should be accomplished during each meeting and checking it against the minutes or with the chair of the board after the meeting.)

- Plan to raise and give money. Regardless of your financial position, this is a key responsibility of being on most boards.

- Make your own financial pledge and gift early in the organization's fiscal year. We guarantee this will endear you to your fellow board members, community, and to the staff.

What you can expect and what's expected of you

■ ■ ■ ■ ■ ■ ■ ■ ■ ■ ■ ■ ■ ■

In return for giving, you can and should expect a lot of satisfaction, joy, and learning. These are not myths. Neither is the feeling of abundance that accompanies giving your time and your money. As in any kind of relationship, however, you are entering into a contract. When you volunteer your time, you are expected to communicate what you need and want, listen to and respect the people to whom you are giving, and follow through on your commitments to them. As you can see from the Volunteer Bill of Rights that follows, you are also entitled to good direction and support.

The volunteer's rights and responsibilities

It Is Your Right

To be assigned a job that is worthwhile and challenging with freedom to use existing skills or develop new ones.

To be trusted with confidential information that will help you carry out your assignment.

To be kept informed through house organs, attendance at staff meetings, memoranda, etc. about what is going on in your organization.

To receive orientation training and supervision for the job you accept and to know why you are asked to do a particular job.

To expect that your time will not be wasted by lack of planning, coordination, or cooperation within your organization.

It Is Your Responsibility

To accept an assignment of your choice with only as much responsibility as you can handle.

To respect confidences of your sponsoring organization and those of the recipients of your services.

To fulfill your commitment or notify your supervisor early enough that a substitute can be found.

To follow guidelines established by organization, codes of dress, decorum, and so on.

To decline work not acceptable to you; not let biases interfere with job performance; not proselytize or pressure recipient to accept your standards. To use time wisely and not interfere with performance of others.

It Is Your Right

To know whether your work is effective and how it can be improved: to have a chance to increase understanding of yourself, others, and your community.

To indicate when you do not want to receive telephone calls or when out-of-pocket costs are too great for you.

To be reimbursed for out-of-pocket costs if it is the only way you can volunteer.

To declare allowable non-reimbursed out-of-pocket costs for federal (some state and local) income-tax purposes if serving with a charitable organization.

To expect valid recommendation and encouragement from your supervisor so you can move to another job—paid or volunteer.

To be given appropriate recognition in the form of awards, certificates of achievement, etc., but even more important, recognition of your day-to-day contributions by other participants in the volunteering relationship.

To ask for a new assignment within your organization.

It Is Your Responsibility

To continue only as long as you can be useful to recipient.

To refuse gifts or tips, except when recipient makes or offers something of nominal value as a way of saying "thank you."

To stipulate limitations: what out-of-pocket costs you can afford, when it is convenient to receive calls from organization or recipient

To use reasonable judgment in making decisions when there appears to be no policy or policy not communicated to you— then, as soon as possible, consult with supervisor for future guidance.

To provide feedback, suggestions, and recommendations to supervisor and staff if these might increase effectiveness of program.

To be considerate, respect competencies, and work as a member of a team with all staff and other volunteers.

Courtesy of San Francisco Volunteer Center

- Be an activist in your board work and treat your board participation as a place to make friends and to expand your skills. If you need more skill in a particular area, take a class for board members (many community colleges have them). The National Center for Nonprofit Boards publishes valuable information and conducts trainings (see Appendix F, Resources).

- Consider what impact you want to have while on the board and discuss your goals and ideas with the board chair. Be prepared to be asked to do more to bring the organization to your vision.

- Take on responsibility to help move the organization forward, always trying to complete tasks you have agreed to do in a timely manner. Think about what would be a transformative contribution. Help the organization think for the future.

- Have most of your communications be with the board chair and committee members. The staff is very busy and board members need to refrain from micro-managing them.

- Do not leave a nonprofit board abruptly. Help create a smooth transition and you will help ensure the future of the organization.

An important volunteer opportunity: Fundraising

Fundraising is the gentle art of teaching the joy of giving.
—Henry A. Rosso, founder, The Fundraising School

One of the most important ways that you can leverage your support for an organization is to volunteer your time and leadership by fundraising. Nonprofit staff don't and cannot raise all of the money they need single-handedly. The money you can bring in by asking others to share your commitment to the work of the organization can far outpace the value of your financial contribution. After all, who better to be asking for money than someone who is giving and enthusiastic enough to ask someone else to give? It is both exciting and satisfying to see the kind of effect you can have this way. In fact, gaining skills and confidence in fundraising makes you a more valuable donor. Being the person asking for funds is also a learning experience, as it gives you a unique perspective on positive and negative donor behavior.

When you are raising money, the best thing you can do is to understand your role as a translator. Your job is to communicate your excitement for the work being done. A lot of material written about fundraising focuses on the nuts and bolts of plans and strategies to raise money. (There are publications and even classes on fundraising. See Appendix F, Resources for starting points.) While these are helpful tools, the essential thing to understand is that fundraising is communication, whether it's in person or in the content or presentation of written materials. If in your fundraising conversations you share your passion about why you are working with a particular organization, you will connect with supporters who believe in and share your mission.

The first step is to recognize that your passion about the organization or project could be catalyzed by multiple reasons. For example, you or a loved one may be or have been a client of the organization; you may be grateful that future beneficiaries of the work of the organization may have better lives; you could be inspired by leaders of the organization; the organization's work could be a manifestation of your spiritual life; you could believe the work is effective; the organization could be a key part of your community.

When fundraising for an organization, place your passion out front. Inspired fundraising reaches beyond asking for money. If you can convey your enthusiasm for the organization to others you will connect on a level of collaboration, where the products of the relationship will transcend what either of you could contribute individually.

What are tangible ways to do this? One way is to complete the exercises in this book that lead you to create your giving plan. Spending time thinking about and planning your giving will help you not only to think about yourself as a donor but also to realize aspects of your giving that you are proud of and others that you would like to change. The executive director of a community foundation, for example, upon working through the book with her partner, was shocked to realize that she hadn't been giving away the 10 percent of her income that she had committed to. She shared this realization and commitment with her board of directors, who were inspired to make their own 10 percent pledges. As a result, their contributions to the organization (and others they believed in) increased.

The pressure to bring funding in can make it hard to keep in touch with your inspiration. Our second recommendation is to recharge your batteries by taking time to connect with program activities of the organization. You could sit in on rehearsals, join a site visit, greet clients at the door, or participate in any number of ways appropriate to the organization you're raising funds for.

The most tangible moment when your translator skills are put to the test is during in-person requests for support. In preparation for talking with a prospective donor, here are some questions to ask yourself that will help you convey your passion along with the need for the organization's mission:

- What drew you to this organization?
- What reminds you of how important it is that you support the organization's work?
- Who are the most inspiring people you've met through your work with this organization? How and why have their lives touched yours?
- Which program stands out as an exciting example of the organization's ability to build community?

If appropriate, share these answers with your prospective donors. Think of the conversation as storytelling. We tell stories to each other to illustrate transformations. You have come to share exciting and inspirational results. In this interchange, the money you are asking for, while it's what has brought the two of you together to talk, becomes a secondary subject. Sharing a passion for the work and the need for the work is the main topic.

Two inspired fundraising stories

The following two stories illustrate what people can do when inspired to raise funds for something that is close to their hearts.

LEE KARA FRIEDLANDER, age 12, noticed that kids in cancer treatment at the local hospital were cut off from friends and family while inpatients. She initiated a request to her local community foundation, the Community Foundation for the Capital Region in Albany, New York, for a laptop computer so kids could e-mail their families and friends. Within just a few weeks, $1,247 was given to the hospital through the foundation for "Write to Cure," providing a laptop to be used by children undergoing treatment at Albany Medical Center's Pediatric Oncology Unit.

TATJANA LOH, a researcher in medical biology, decided she wanted to help raise money for battered women's shelters. Realizing she would need training in fundraising, she adopted a hands-on approach, volunteering several hours each week as assistant to the executive director of a local nonprofit. There she helped with fundraising tasks while learning the basic skills of the job. She then became an intern with a battered women's shelter where she received training on how to write grants and plan events. Though these two learning experiences required a good deal of Tatjana's time, her commitment paid off: she became an excellent fundraiser. She went on to a position as executive director of a coalition of battered women's shelters, raising more than $150,000 a year.

Over the years, and because she took the time to learn a much-needed skill, Tatjana has become a valuable volunteer on committees, member of boards, and staff person in the nonprofit sector.

Chapter 7

Where to give, and how

▪ ▪ ▪

The giving plan that you will complete in Chapter Eight will lay out the elements to accomplish your mission. This chapter covers the first steps of developing your giving plan, including how to find information about specific groups to give to and how to decide which are worthy of your time and dollars.

One of the first steps in writing your plan is to identify the main areas of interest you want to fund based on your assessment of their strategic importance. This framework narrows where you decide to commit your time, talents, and treasures. It gives you immediate criteria for the financial and/or time commitments that are and are not going to be part of your giving.

Choosing where to give

With more than 1.6 million nonprofits in the United States alone, how many do we really know about? Do you only know about the big national groups that get your attention with their direct mail appeals and community billboards? What if you've decided you want to support groups responding to local problems in your community, or you've heard about some regional or statewide groups that sound interesting? Or maybe you're wondering if the groups you already give to are really the ones you want to continue to support?

Most people have these questions. One of the benefits of creating your giving plan is taking the time to think seriously about where your financial contributions will have the greatest impact on the issues you care most about.

In many cases a percentage of your giving will be gifts that support cherished or honored obligations and civic responsibilities. The question is how much of your giving are you committed to making more strategic or transformational in proposed outcomes for the world or community at large. It will take discipline and added time to find leaders and groups that can accomplish your goals, as most people fund projects they have been involved with or that their friends tell them about or ask them to support. But the satisfaction of moving beyond all obligatory gifts to ones you feel more passionate about can be life-changing and world-changing.

Sources of information

To think about which groups you want to include in your giving, use Exercise 7.1 to list your top priority interest areas and compare that to the list of groups you currently give to from Exercise 3.1 (Chapter Three). Do your gifts reflect your top interest areas? Do you wonder if there are other groups also working in these areas that you don't yet know about? Are you thinking only about local groups? Would donating to statewide, national, or international organizations achieve additional important strategic goals? What if the most effective model is found internationally? You might start by asking friends, family and colleagues which organizations they support. Beyond such an informal survey, finding out about what groups exist that address the issues you care most about takes a little research.

In the human service field, to add to any groups you already know about, you can contact your nearest United Way office or alternative fund or federation for a list of groups they fund (for these and other ideas mentioned in this section, see Appendix F, Resources). For issues outside of human services, your local or statewide community foundation, Funding Exchange member fund, or women's foundation or federation can provide information about groups serving your community. Or try an online giving portal site that can connect you to organizations that may match your interest areas or be within the geographic limits you have prioritized. These resources are helpful if you're just beginning to identify what kinds

Your Funding Areas

20 minutes

Step 1. Write your mission statement from Exercise 4.1 in Chapter Four.

Mission Statement:

_____

_____

_____

_____

Step 2. Write the total amount of money you've decided to give and the amount of time you plan to volunteer.

Total Giving Plan for _____ (year)

Financial donations: _____

Volunteering: _____

Step 3. Look at your mission statement. Think about concrete work and strategies that will make it a reality. It may help to look back at the work you did in Chapter Two on identifying your top priority interest areas (Exercise 2.3), though these may have changed as a result of the subsequent exercises. It will also help to review the exercises you did in Chapter Three: the characteristics of your past funding (Exercise 3.1) and your analysis of creating a better world (Exercises 3.2 and 3.3).

Now list no more than five areas of funding. Limiting yourself to five main areas, or fewer, perhaps three, will help to maintain focus and attention.

Areas of Funding

1. _____

2. _____

3. _____

4. _____

5. _____

Step 4. Now think about whether prioritizing your choices will make your strategy more effective. If so, rewrite your list in priority order.

Areas of Funding

1. _____

2. _____

3. _____

4. _____

5. _____

Step 5. From the total amount of money you've decided to donate, allocate a percentage to each area based on your assessment in Step 4 of the importance of each to your mission. Then translate each percentage into a dollar amount. For an example, see the sample giving plan for $8,400 in Chapter Eight. The family's strongest interest is in civil rights, so they allocate 47 percent of their giving budget to civil rights groups. They're also concerned about death and dying and alternative medical and spiritual care, so 30 percent of their giving goes to organizations whose missions are in this area. Their final area of interest is educational opportunity and support, so they give 23 percent of their financial donations to literacy and other educational endeavors.

Final Areas of Funding (in priority order if applicable)

	Amount	Percentage
1. _____	_____	_____
2. _____	_____	_____
3. _____	_____	_____
4. _____	_____	_____
5. _____	_____	_____

of things you might want to fund or need more information about a specific non-profit.

You can also learn more about specific nonprofits from a growing number of private monitoring groups, such as the National Charities Information Bureau, the Philanthropic Advisory Service of the Better Business Bureau, and the American Institute of Philanthropy. Each of these groups reviews financial and fiduciary performance of nonprofits. Philanthropic Research, Inc. also publishes reports on thousands of organizations.

Gathering information

One of the best ways to understand an issue or cause and learn about what's being done about it is by getting information from groups or leaders working on the topic. These groups and leaders will have different expertise, information, and perspective about the issue that will expand your own knowledge and help you make giving choices most appropriate for you.

As you find specific groups you may want to donate to, contact them for their newsletters or annual reports. When available, an annual report will describe the agency's mission and its goals and objectives for the previous year and how they were met; it will also convey the agency's perception of its impact and effectiveness. By law, you may also request a group's tax report, called a "990 Form," which will reveal the percentage of gifts and income spent on administration, program, and fundraising. The Web site www.guidestar.org makes available the 990 tax forms of more than 850,000 nonprofits. Though the rule of thumb is that not more than 25 percent of an organization's budget should go to fundraising and administration, start-up agencies or those doing work that has never been done, or work that is highly risky or complex may initially need up to 40 percent or even more of the charitable dollars they receive to be spent on infrastructure, (staffing, administration, operating expenses, and the like). We urge you to focus first on the content, constituency, and quality of the work and then look at the group's budget and finances.

Getting even closer, you might want to attend events a group sponsors. Or you can volunteer with a group that particularly interests you and is based locally to get a sense of its program and leadership, the strength of the executive director and other staff, the board and their experience, and the size and structure of the volunteer corps. If you become a major donor to a group (depending on the size of the group, a $100 gift may be considered major or only gifts of $5,000 or more), you can expect that a board of staff member will seek to meet with you to give you updates about the group's work. If you are considering making a substantial donation, we highly recommend that you review the organization's current and projected budgets. You may also want to conduct a site visit. Guidelines for reviewing budgets and making site visits are in Chapter Twelve.

Different organizations work differently, even on the same issues. Table 7.1 presents some notion of the variety of strategies that groups and organizations can apply in working on issues, with particular attention to the relationship of donors to each strategy. Different strategies result in different activities to create change. Use the chart to find strategies that seem the best choices for meeting your personal mission statement and that you feel most comfortable giving to, given the funding considerations discussed here. Using multiple strategies over a five- to twenty-year period is often the best way to see and create change.

Giving internationally

Many of the compelling and challenging issues in philanthropy today are global in nature and international in scope. Charity may begin at home, but it doesn't end there. As private investment capital profits from "emerging markets," so private philanthropic capital discovers "emerging opportunities" when it goes abroad. Because it is efficient giving, small donations can yield big results.

Giving internationally can be a valuable way to help remedy some serious difficulties people and the environment face in some other countries, particularly poverty; impeded economic development; the negative results of globalization; limited access to schooling; poor health care; and economic, racial, and gender inequalities.

According to *Giving USA 2001,* private American giving abroad amounts to less than 2 percent of the country's total private giving, and governmental giving from post-industrialized countries has been shrinking. It only makes sense that as the world is increasingly interconnected, so that even what we wear and eat are enmeshed in the flow of international capital, goods, services, and labor, we attend to the grassroots needs of those whose work contributes to our welfare. Solutions to some of the world's great problems will and have been resolved by international collaborations.

A number of international agencies direct donations overseas. Many have offices or staff in the United States, as well as advisors, partner organizations, offices, or consultants overseas. These on-site intermediary organizations are well connected and full of great information about local politics and strategic ideas about what needs funding (see Resources). We also urge you to visit the Web site www.internationaldonors.org, managed by Grantmakers Without Borders, for information and resources about international giving.

Making decisions

The basis for your decision making about where to give is finding matches between your mission and the missions of the organizations you are considering. In order to do that, you need to know how an organization works to accomplish its mission and how effective its work is.

Two remaining factors involved in your decision making are risk and trust. Like good decision making about a lot of things, a certain amount of action in this area involves daring to make decisions that either might not turn out as you hope or, conversely, may yield more than anyone could have imagined. If your tolerance for risk is low, think about challenging yourself. Since what's at stake can potentially change lives, the returns can be huge.

Risk and trust involve recognizing that philanthropy is a collaboration. The act of giving money, time, or attention, engages us with others and creates community. Giving trust and reliability builds these bonds. You may not need to know everything about an issue you care about or about the organizations working on it in order to make a thoughtful funding decision. For many donations, as a donor you may be satisfied having a general sense of trust in an organization's effectiveness and

Table 7.1 Commonly Used Strategies for Change, Relationship to Donors, and Considerations.

STRATEGY	Charity: Social Service	Coalition Building	Empowerment	Advocacy/Social Change/ Transformational Philanthropy
WHAT IT DOES	Provides imme-diate support for individuals and families in need.	A network of services or a system of organi-zations focus on one issue or social prob-lem.	An adjunct component of delivering services that positively affects the capacity of a person or group of people to help themselves.	Works to change systems and address the roots of disadvantage. Advocates for public policies or wide-spread behavior change.
TYPES OF ACTIVITIES	• Disaster relief • Soup kitchens • Food banks • Emergency housing • Healthcare	• A hospital or other healthcare delivery system • A disaster relief system • A network of serv-ices serving home-less youth	• Economic development • Youth recreation with leadership, civic, or per-sonal development • Supporting a group to find collective strength or identity • Scholarships or training • Direct action where par-ticipants gain valuable skills	• Grassroots organizing and public education (including media education) • Action-oriented think tanks • Media education campaigns • Public policy reform • Global networking via the Internet
DONOR RELATIONSHIP	Donor funds a service provider or other agency that gives money or goods to individuals	Donor funds intermedi-ary that links and helps manage network or service providers of the affected groups.	Donor funds organizations or intermediaries providing the services.	A funder or group of funders support a coali-tion or group.
CONSIDERATIONS	Immediate good feel-ing for the donor and relief to the needy, but sustained impact may depend on longer-term strategies.	Can be difficult to evaluate effective-ness. Coalitions and true collaborations take a great deal of time and may take staffing to maximize results.	Results are generally uneven and difficult to ascertain; those that can be seen are often very helpful and gratifying.	Work is complex and needs advisory resources and national or interna-tional contacts or considerations.

Expanded from a chart by Stephanie Clohesy

Venture Philanthropy and Market Models	Building Infrastructure	Electoral Politics and Campaign Reform	Grassroots Community Organizing	Prayer, Meditation, and Reflection
Provides strategic assistance for entrepreneurial endeavors (often bridging nonprofit and for-profit work) that combine innovative solutions with sustainability plans.	Stabilizes organizations through underwriting core operating, building, planning, marketing, or development expenses.	Enables democratic process through public education, voter polling, education, electoral, or campaign reform.	Educates and mobilizes constituencies and supporters to create change.	Funds organizations, leaders, or congregations to enable greater societal reflection, conflict resolution, or spiritual direction
• Business that supports a nonprofit activity, such as used clothing • Business training center • Agency that provides low-interest loans for small business or social entrepreneurial efforts • A cluster of organizations that share resources or network and are often located in one building or share space	• Rent, building or land purchase • Staff or development consultants • Strategic planning process or consultants • Media or public relations campaign	• Voter education to particular populations or geographic areas • Campaign finance reform • Party campaign literature or media messaging or ads • Gifts to a political party • Support or volunteering for public protests or direct action • Art that makes a political statement	• Phone or door-to-door educators or organizers • Direct action or protest • Art or culture with a message • Media, the Internet, or research	• Conflict resolution • Prayer circles • Peace vigils • Retreat centers • Supporting spiritual or cultural leaders • Programs or training such as meditation in prisons or workplaces • Inspirational materials or campaigns to ask the public to reflect on or change behaviors
Donor or group of donors provide grants or investments. High engagement and monitoring for success.	Usually direct between funder and the nonprofit project	Funder often asked to give money early and to weather ethical considerations of current and ever-changing political environment. Not all gifts deductible.	Donors must be sensitive to issues of domination and class differences in order to build strong partnerships with grassroots organizations.	Funders are often members of a congregation or giving circle, or may give anonymously through intermediary organizations or leaders.
Nonprofit and for-profit consultants and board and staff with business experience needed. Adequate capital and sound fiscal and management experience key.	Need to establish realistic objectives and outcomes.	Direct action is a key tool for civil engagement and democratic functioning. Funds may be used for high overhead. Some results hard to evaluate. Win or lose situations. Direct action, lobbying or protesting can be challenging. Training is advised.	Typically low salaries result in high staff, turnover which can affect outcomes.	Results are sometimes less apparent externally and often long term. Approaches may not seem to address root causes but may work on attitudes, which is at the root of most change

leadership and not need to know more. For others, you may want to have an indepth working knowledge of the group. The decision about your level of comfort on this score is your own.

Exercise 7.2 contains a set of questions to ask yourself and groups you are considering giving to in order to help you to determine whether your donation to the group is effective for you in fulfilling your mission.

Evaluating How an Organization Meets Your Goals and How You Meet Its Goals

45 minutes

You may need to complete this exercise in two stages. First, answer all the questions that you can based on what you know and any materials you have from the organization, such as a fundraising letter or proposal and general informational materials. If you have unanswered questions at that point, you may need to talk to someone at the organization.

1. **Mission:** What are the stated goals of the project or organization I am considering giving to? Do they seem realistic? How do they fit with the following aspects of my giving plan?

   _____

   _____

   _____

2. **Strategy:** How is this project working on the needs it is addressing? Does the work seem to be effective—that is, are the strategy and the actions to carry out that strategy contributing to change in the desired direction? Does this program or group reach the people I want to have an effect on? Are enough people reached?

   _____

   _____

   _____

3. **Impact:** What impact will my giving money or time to this program, person, or group have? How much of a difference will it make? Is this a small group that my donation will have a large impact on? Or a large group that it will have moderate impact on?

   _____

   _____

   _____

4. **Time:** What is the short-term outcome of this work projected to be? What long-term outcome is projected?

_____

_____

_____

5. **Timeliness:** Does this project need to be funded now? What would the impact be if it were shelved for a while?

_____

_____

_____

6. **Type of donation:** Will this be a donation (tax-deductible or not)? A no-interest loan?

_____

_____

_____

7. **Volunteer time?** What will my role be?

_____

_____

_____

8. **Decision-making:** Do I have the information I need to make a thoughtful decision?

_____

_____

_____

9. **Alternative prospects:** Are there other places or ways that this group or project could receive the funding they are asking of me? Is it possible for them to do so?

_____

_____

Chapter 8

Creating your personal giving plan

■ ■ ■

You have now reached the heart of *Inspired Philanthropy*—writing your Personal Giving Plan. Let's review what you've done so far. You've been introduced to the world of philanthropy, the who and why of giving, the differences between traditional and inspired philanthropy, and the benefits of being an organized giver. You've taken an inventory of your current position as a donor or potential donor, identified your passions as a giver, and written your personal mission statement. You've assessed how you currently spend your time and money and, given your interests and vision, how you would like to allocate those resources in the future.

Now it's time to make a plan for how, where, and when to distribute the funds you've decided to contribute. (Even if you don't have a formal budget, Exercise 5.2 in Chapter Five should have given you a sense of how much you want to give, either as an absolute figure or as a percentage of your annual income.) In this chapter, you'll draft your giving plan and create your funding cycles, deciding when during the year you want to make—and make good on—funding decisions. This chapter also includes tools to assess the results and impact of your giving.

When you've created and tried out your personal giving plan you'll find that it not only helps you manage your planned contributions, it also allows you to anticipate unexpected requests and engage in spontaneous acts of whimsy or demonstrations of caring. A personal giving plan can also help you organize your time, so that you spend it in ways that reflect your values.

The worksheet

In the following pages you'll find a Giving Plan worksheet (Worksheet 8.1) and examples of completed plans (Tables 8.1 through 8.5). (While the sample plans include the names of actual nonprofits, all other names are fictitious and the examples composites, offered for thought and discussion, not as ideals.) You may want to make a few copies of the blank worksheet to work from or create one for yourself on a computer so you can generate copies as you need them. Spend some time looking at the sample completed forms, then try filling one out yourself, guided by the steps outlined in Exercise 8.1.

This is one of the most important worksheets in this book, so give it as much time as you need.

The first time through, just do it as an exercise, without necessarily committing yourself to the results. Try to fill out every column in one session. By doing this you'll find out where you need more information or aren't yet ready to make decisions. You may find you need to refer back to earlier chapters or do more research on your own.

Once you've filled in any gaps in your thinking as best you can, fill out a clean copy of the Giving Plan, creating a working document you can use. Refer to the sample giving plans that follow Worksheet 8.1 to see how others at various income levels and with various funding interests have created their giving plans.

Congratulations! You have completed your first year's Giving Plan. Take a look at it and see how it feels. Make any adjustments you want before you start implementing it, and then make a commitment to yourself to follow the plan for the next year.

Your Personal Giving Plan

Mission Statement: _____

_____

_____

Total Giving Plan for (year): _____   Financial donations: _____   Volunteering: _____

Area of Funding	Percentage	Amount	Specific Groups or Questions to Research	Amount per Group	Volunteer Hours	Funding Cycle	Notes, Contacts, Previous Gifts

Your Giving Plan

30 minutes or more

The plan you create should cover one year, starting now. Once you have a plan drafted, try it out for the whole twelve months and then evaluate and refine as necessary. Use a copy of the blank Giving Plan (Worksheet 8.1) that follows to do this exercise.

Step 1. *Transfer the answers to Exercise 7.1 in Chapter Seven to your draft Giving Plan,* including your mission statement, the total amount of money you've decided to give, and your areas of funding and volunteering.

If there are other areas you want to include, such as gifts to family and friends and tickets to fundraising events and dinners, add them here. You may also want to include a miscellaneous category, where you give yourself room to make spontaneous or whimsical gifts, and where you can respond to good work and urgent needs that may require a quick reaction. There are moments in history when we are simply called to consider different approaches or engage in spontaneous acts of heartfelt (inspired) giving. These are instances when timing and societal change converge. For example, if violence were to break out in your city or town, you might want to make a donation to help support conflict resolution efforts, or volunteer some hours if you have skills that could help.

Step 2. *On the basis of the research you did in Chapter Seven, where possible, designate specific groups you want to give to.* If you haven't decided on all the groups you may want to include in a particular funding area, place a question mark where you need more information (see the sample individual giving plan for $2,500 in this chapter). The goals of the groups you choose should help accomplish your own giving mission. Think here about the balance of small, medium, and large organizations and the distribution of local, statewide, regional, national, and international groups.

This one step will immediately help you to deal with the many requests that come in the mail or on the phone. If a request would fit in this column, consider it. If it doesn't but it still speaks to one of your values, consider whether you want to give to it through your miscellaneous whimsy category. If neither is the case, throw it away.

Step 3. *Indicate dollar amounts you will give to each group.* If there's more than one group you want to give to in a given area, think about how you want to distribute the amount of money you've allocated to this area among the groups you've listed. There are some strategic points to consider for each organization: Would your dollars be most effective to the organization in a large or small gift? If you can do so, making a large gift of $250 to $5,000 may be crucial to the survival of some fledgling organizations. A local group may do more with $100 than a national organization can do with $500. For some colleges and high schools with multi-million-dollar capital campaigns, alumni participation at any level may be more important than the size of the gift.

Experiment with different amounts and give yourself permission to make mistakes with gifts. If you learn that something you did wasn't right, you'll find out more clearly what does suit you.

Step 4. *Decide how much time you want to volunteer in each area.* In the column for Volunteer Hours, write in a number of hours per week or month you would like to donate as a volunteer for particular groups. Your volunteer time may also go to organizations you do not support financially. (Add these to the list of groups within each area of funding.)

Also, decide if you're going to volunteer on a regular basis—say, a weekly stint answering phones or attending a monthly board meeting—or a seasonal basis—say, planning a fundraising event or helping write grant proposals at certain times of the year.

Step 5. *Decide on your funding cycles.* When are you going to make your funding decisions and write your checks: will you do it once, twice, or four times a year; in the spring, the fall, at the New Year, on your birthday? Or will you decide whenever asked? In choosing your cycles you might consider times of the year you have a tight cash flow, tax time, heavy request times, and times when dinners and events seem to cluster. Once you've decided when you'll give, give yourself permission not to make any gifts outside of your giving cycles. Write the date of your funding cycles at the top of the column, and then write in when you plan to write a check or otherwise give to a group.

Step 6. *Add any relevant notes.* Use the notes column to record names of contacts, previous gifts you made to this group, or other information pertinent to your gifts of money and time. This might include information such as whether the gift is to an organization with local, regional, national, or international reach, which strategy the work is focusing on, and other choices you have made.

TABLE 8.1 Sample Individual Giving Plan—$2,500.

Mission Statement: I believe that education fosters personal growth and change. I aim to fund individuals, including nonprofit leaders, and provide tuition funding for educational or renewal opportunities.

Total Giving Plan for 2003: Financial donations: $1500 to nonprofits, $1,000 to political activities and $500 in value of donated items. This totals just under 6 percent of my income ($41,000). **Volunteering:** About four hours each week, most of it at the kids' school.

Area of Funding	Percentage	Amount	Specific Groups or Questions to Research	Amount per Group	Volunteer Hours	Funding Cycle	Notes, Contacts, Previous Gifts
Retreats for leaders, low-income people, friends	Approximately 24%	$700	Massachusetts Jobs with Justice Coalition	$400	25	June	Retreats to build Western Mass. organizing networks
			?_____ need to research	$200			
Leadership Development	Approximately 20%	$500	Appalachian Women's Leadership Project	$300		December	Talked with Patrick about keeping this anonymous
			American Friends Service Committee, Youth Empowerment Project	$200		June	
Education and scholarships for individuals	Approximately 8%	$200	Science Enrichment Program at Kids' school	$100	200	September	For Chris Sampieri. Send check directly to school for tax deduction.
			Towards Josh's tuition	$100		October	
Donor's Whim: Miscellaneous Gifts, Social Events	Approximately 8%	$200	Penn State class gift for international student fund	$100		April	Call class rep re challenge for scholarship fund
			Middle East Crisis Committee	$50		December	
			Project Hip Hop	$50		December	
Political Gifts—Non-deductible	Approximately 20%	$500	School Board Candidate	$250		April	
			Candidate for Governor	$250		April	
Political Gifts—Deductible	Approximately 20%	$500	White House Project	$250		April	Media fund
			League of Women Voters	$250		June	For Roxbury voter registration project
In-kind Gifts			Habitat for Humanity	$250 value	25	June	
			Clothes for yard sale for women's shelter	$150 value		October	
			Auction item for River Project	$150 value		December	

TABLE 8.2 Sample Family Giving Plan—$8,400.

Mission Statement: We deeply value helping others because no one should have to face all of life's ups and downs alone. Taking care of our elderly parents has also moved us to want to change conditions of death and dying.

Total Giving Plan for 2003: Financial donations: $8,400 (7 percent of our family pretax income of $120 000). **Volunteering:** Four hours each week for each of us, including the kids (about 800 hours this year as a family).

Area of Funding	Percentage	Amount	Specific Groups or Questions to Research	Amount per Group	Volunteer Hours	Funding Cycle	Notes, Contacts, Previous Gifts
Civil Rights	Approximately 47%	$3,950	NAACP	$500		January	
			Black United Fund	$2,080		all year	$40/week x 52 weeks from payroll deduction
			Southern Poverty Law Center	$450		September	For anti-racism film
			Delta Sigma Theta sorority	$370	100	January	Newsletter subscription
			Center for Democratic Renewal	$50		January	
			Grassroots Leadership	$500		January	
Death and Dying; Alternative and Spiritual Care	Approximately 30%	$2,450	Atlanta Hospice	$500		January	In honor of Eulenia Heinz in memory of Nellie Lorance
			Make-a-Wish Foundation	$250		October	
			Commonwheel	$500	200	October	
			Center for Alternative Treatment & Care	$1,200		October	$25/week for service and care
Educational Opportunity and Support	Approximately 23%	$2,000	Literacy Education Fund of Atlanta	$1,000	100	January	Summer program volunteer hours
			Highlander Center	$300	100	October	
			Mothers Against Drunk Drivers	$50		January	Membership
			Ebenezer Baptist Church	$150	300	April	
			research best nonprofit—call Julio at Comm. Fnd.	$500			

TABLE 8.3 Sample Family Giving Plan—$26,000.

Mission Statement: We seek to encourage full participation in local agencies in the two communities in which we live (Easthampton and New York City).

Total Giving Plan for 2003: Financial donations: $26,000 (10 percent of family pretax income of $260,000).
Volunteering: Three hours for each of us each week (total of 500 hours per year).

Area of Funding	Percentage	Amount	Specific Groups or Questions to Research	Amount per Group	Volunteer Hours	Funding Cycle	Notes, Contacts, Previous Gifts
Nature/Beauty/ Environment	Approxi- mately 44%	$11,500	Botanical Gardens, NYC	$7,500	300	January	In honor of Suzie Williams
			The Nature Conservancy	$1,000		January	In honor of Jordan's birthday
			Trees Foundation	$1,000		June	
			Central Park Foundation	$2,000		June	
Health	Approxi- mately 29%	$7,500	Southampton Hospital	$2,000		June	In honor of John
			Lighthouse for the Blind	$1,000		June	
			Long Island Food Bank	$1,500		December	For the storage building fund
			NY Food Bank	$3,000		December	
Education and Opportunity	Approxi- mately 27%	$7,000	Boys Club of New York	$4,000	100	December	Table at annual dinner
			Long Island Public Radio	$1,000	100	June	For summer youth intern
			Planned Parenthood	$1,500		December	
			Madeline Island Library	$1,000		December	In honor of Agnes Cadotte

TABLE 8.4 Sample Family Giving Plan—$45,000.

Mission Statement: We believe that communities should preserve their cultural heritage. We fund the arts and new uses of technology because we believe they are the most effective methods to document, preserve, and perpetuate culture. We give anonymously through our donor-advised fund at the Seattle Community Foundation.

Total Giving Plan for 2003: Financial donations: $45,000 (15 percent of family pretax income of $360,000).
Volunteering: Three hours each week, both of us (300 hours per year).

Area of Funding	Percentage	Amount	Specific Groups or Questions to Research	Amount per Group	Volunteer Hours	Funding Cycle	Notes, Contacts, Previous Gifts
Cultural Arts	50%	$22,500	Asian Arts Museum	$5,000		November	
			Asian Cultural Center	$5,000		November	
			Public Library	$2,200		March	
			Asian Elders Oral History Project	$10,000	100	March	For CD-ROM; talked to Alice Ito
Education and Technology	25%	$11,250	Educational Fund for Bilingual Teachers	$5,000		March	
			Stanford University	$1,250		November	
			The International Forum on Globalization	$5,000		November	Web site development
Philanthropy and Volunteerism	25%	$11,250	Social Venture Partners, Seattle	$5,000	200	March	For regranting with high-tech peers
			United Way	$1,250		March	
			A Territory Resource	$5,000		March	

TABLE 8.5 Sample Individual Giving Plan—$200,000.

Mission Statement: I commit to help Colorado become a state of opportunity for all, with respect to all races, ethnicities, lifestyles and economic backgrounds. I want to help reinvigorate the debate on issues affecting the well-being of families and working adults while promoting public policies that open gateways to a more fully functioning democracy.

Total Giving Plan for 2003: Financial donations: $200,000 (8% of family pretax income of $1,250,000 and 1% assets of $10,000,000). **Volunteering:** 400 hours per year.

Area of Funding	Percentage	Amount	Specific Groups or Questions to Research	Amount per Group	Volunteer Hours	Funding Cycle	Notes, Contacts, Previous Gifts
Policy and Advocacy	50%	$100,000	Bell Policy Center	$90,000	200	March	
			Institute for Policy Studies	$10,000		December	
Community Service and Civic Responsibility	30%	$60,000	Women's Fund of Colorado	$20,000	50	March	
			The Bean Project	$20,000	50	March	
			Boulder Community Foundation	$20,000		July	
Global and National Opportunities and Innovations	20%	$40,000	Changemakers	$10,000	100	July	
			Global Fund for Women	$20,000		July	
			Sierra Club Legal Defense Fund	$10,000		December	

Clarifying your intention

As you begin to make your gifts, you may want to ground yourself even further in your intentions for them. Knowing what your intention is will also help later when you evaluate whether the gifts were effective.

You may want to copy Worksheet 8.2 so you can fill it out for each gift that you intend to evaluate (it takes only a few minutes to complete) and file it as a reminder of your own intention at the time of the giftgiving.

Results and impact: Giftmaking yearly review

There is much to learn by implementing your giving plan. Once you've completed your year of giftmaking, or as often as you want to do so, reflect on how well your money was used and how well you feel you did as a donor.

Worksheets 8.3 and 8.4 that follow provide questions that may be useful in your review.

A multi-year giving plan as in Table 8.6 (followed by Worksheet 8.5, a blank form you can reproduce and use) can be a simple and helpful way to look at what you've been doing and plan ahead.

Expanding your giving horizon

> Philanthropy is commendable, but it must not cause the philanthropist to over-look the circumstances of economic injustice that make philanthropy necessary.
>
> —Dr. Martin Luther King, Jr.

> It is not enough to be compassionate. You must act.
>
> —The Dalai Lama

Having a giving plan is an important tool. It's one step in responding to the enormous problems that create inequality and violence and illness for millions of people every day. It's hard to conceive that your donations, whether $500 or $50,000 a year, will really make much of a dent in the vast web of those problems. Yet through conscientious, thoughtful responses, the donations of each person contribute to positive change. Here is what some experienced donors have said:

I know that my donations combine with thousands of others to make change and help people daily. Given my privilege, that is enough. My job is to admit my place in society's current order and to do my part to share what I can. Of hundreds of contributions I have made, fewer than 1 percent have, I think, been spent without adequate care or expertise. Trusting others to know what needs to be done and giving them the chance to do so is my task.

■　　■　　■

I see that the steady and intentional gifts I have made over time have built organizational stability and leadership savvy.

■　　■　　■

Having a giving plan has opened my eyes to what is around me and, through the choices it requires me to make, has made me more reverent of the multitude of worthy needs and more angry about the addictions and narrowness of the material world.

■　　■　　■

I have learned never to resist my own generous impulses.

Giving Intention

Name of organization: _____

Date of gift: _____ Amount of gift: $_____

With this gift/donation, I want to participate in

_____ The spirit of generosity and faith

_____ Supporting someone I trust or respect

_____ Sustaining the mission of an organization I believe in

_____ Working with other donors or nonprofit leaders

_____ Increasing the financial capacity of an organization

_____ Helping to leverage more resources through a challenge gift

_____ Advancing leadership capacity within an organization through money or time given expressly for trainings

_____ Providing support for direct services to constituents

_____ Helping to provide specific outreach or support to a targeted population or a specific geographic area

_____ Assisting to ensure that the issues being addressed by this organization or leaders get media or PR exposure

_____ Providing tangible goods (clothes, computers, desks, food)

_____ Assuring public policy or advocacy linkages

_____ Designating money for research or documentation

_____ Helping a group or community do better planning, visioning, or collaborating

_____ Contributing to public education options

_____ Funding an artistic presentation, interpretation, or expression

_____ Attaining visibility or recognition for our family or business

_____ Other: _____

_____

For gifts of more than $5,000

1. The organization and I have set detailed goals or agreed on the expected impact of my gift: Yes   No

   Comments/notes:

   _____

   _____

   _____

   _____

2. At the time of my gift I specified how and if I wanted to be recognized.

   I was specific with _____ (person's name) at _____ (name of organization) about my wish to remain anonymous; we spoke on _____ (date) in person / phone /
   in writing (attach letter to file).

   I do not wish to remain anonymous.

   Comments/notes:

   _____

   _____

   _____

   _____

3. I spoke with _____ (person's name) in the organization on _____ (date)
   about reports I do and do not want to receive on the organization's work.

   Example: "I spoke with Jody Stella on July 16th about the fact that I only wish to receive the annual
   report and one call or visit a year."

   Comments/notes:

   _____

   _____

   _____

   _____

   _____

Results and Impact

If you gave large gifts that you want to evaluate before giving again, answer the following questions about the impact of your donation:

1. What were my intentions and goals and were they reached? (Have I reviewed the organization's finances or received a report about how the money was spent? Was my donation spent as it was intended, designated, or originally requested? If not, was I informed along the way?)

_____

_____

_____

2. What do I perceive is the organization's progress and what tools can I use for evaluation? What other organizations collaborated or worked on this issue? What feedback could I get from them about the effectiveness of the group I gave to? (For large gifts: Do I want to hire someone to do a more formal evaluation or do it myself?)

_____

_____

_____

3. How stable does the leadership seem now? Is it stronger? Weaker?

_____

_____

_____

4. Is the organization more, or less, financially stable now?

_____

_____

_____

_____

5. Were there strategic outcomes—programs, products, or services?

_____

_____

_____

_____

6. Did the gift leverage other money or results?

_____

_____

_____

_____

7. How do I feel about administrative costs versus program and fundraising costs at this organization now? Are they different than I expected?

_____

_____

_____

_____

8. What learning went on for me and for the organization through this gift, if any?

_____

_____

_____

_____

Notes about future gifts or about concerns or feedback to share with group or leader:

_____

_____

_____

How You Did as a Donor

Take a few minutes to recall your giving and volunteering over the past year. Check any of the items below that describe your activities. Then go through the checklist again and put a star next to anything you would like to do differently in the coming year.

Volunteering

I volunteered each week/month (check one)

_____ 1–2 hours

_____ 3–5 hours

_____ 6–10 hours

_____ 11–16 hours

_____ 17–20 hours

_____ 21+ hours

I volunteered with the following organizations and did the following activities:

_____

_____

_____

_____

_____

_____

_____

_____

_____

I increased my ability to assist the nonprofit sector by

_____ taking a class (for example, how to be a board member, fundraising, other skills)

_____ reading about nonprofit or community issues

_____ other: _____

Fundraising

I leveraged my ability to support organizations by

_____ learning about fundraising

_____ fundraising from individuals

_____ hosting events for nonprofits or politicians

_____ co-hosting large events (e.g., buying a table of seats and organizing friends to come)

_____ speaking as a donor at events to motivate others to give

_____ speaking to media about my giving

_____ other: _____

Giving

I gave

_____ small amounts to many groups

_____ larger amounts to several groups

_____ a balance of the two

I gave to

_____ too many groups

_____ enough groups

_____ not enough groups

As a percentage of income or assets I gave

_____ adequately

_____ less than I could have

_____ more than I could really afford

I collected mail requests and gave to selected ones

_____ as they came in

_____ monthly

_____ quarterly

_____ yearly

_____ not at all

I attended fundraising events

_____ once or twice

_____ quarterly

_____ monthly

_____ more often

_____ not at all

I generally gave

_____ anonymously

_____ using my name

_____ publicly if asked

I gave to the following number of issues or populations:

_____ 1–2

_____ 3–4

_____ 5–6

I evaluated where to give by

_____ reading annual reports, funding proposals, or direct mail pieces

_____ going on site visits or talking to staff

_____ attending briefings on the issues I give to

_____ talking to other funders and activists

_____ checking with groups that evaluate nonprofits

_____ listening to my heart

_____ other: _____

Planning

I followed an overall giving plan that named how much I would give of

_____ income

_____ assets

_____ time

My giving plan specified

_____ my areas of focus

_____ the types of organizations and strategies I want to support

I reflected on my overall giving

_____ at the beginning or end of the year

_____ on a regular basis during the year (how often?)

_____ through drawing, writing, or talking with others

_____ through a formal evaluation process

I talked or consulted with the following people about my philanthropy

_____ a financial planner or investment manager

_____ an estate attorney

_____ a friend or fellow donor

_____ a mentor or philanthropic advisor

_____ a development director

_____ foundation staff

_____ an activist involved in the areas I give to

_____ a donor support network

_____ other: _____

Identity and Community

I let others know I am

_____ a donor/giver/philanthropist

_____ a volunteer or activist

_____ a donor activist or donor organizer

I made some of my giving decisions

_____ with others (partner, family, friends)

_____ by talking with other donors who give to what I do

_____ with support of a donor network or giving club

_____ other: _____

Integration of Values

In addition to giving and volunteering, I expressed my values by

_____ loaning money to nonprofit organizations

_____ investing in socially responsible companies

_____ investing in community development loan funds and microenterprise funds

_____ practicing ways to live more simply

_____ protesting policies I don't believe in

_____ voting to get things changed or to preserve what I think is just

_____ other: _____

Overall I feel _____ about my giving plan and process.

Next year I want to _____

_____

_____

_____

_____

_____

_____

_____

_____

_____

_____

_____

_____

_____

_____

_____

_____

_____

_____

_____

Table 8.6 Sample Multi-Year Giving Plan.

Area of Funding	Organization	2003	2004	2005	2006	2007	2008
Civil Rights	Black United Fund	$2,080	$2,100				
	NAACP	$500	$500	$500 pledge			
	Grassroots Leadership	$500	$500				
	Southern Poverty Law Center	$450	$450	$500 pledge			
	Delta Sigma Theta sorority	$370	$400				
	Center for Democratic Renewal	$50	$50				
Death and Dying: Alternative and Spiritual Care	Center for Alternative Treatment and Care	$1,200	$1,200				
	Atlanta Hospice	$500	$500				
	Commonwheel Center	$500	$500				
	Make-a-Wish Foundation	$250	(deleted)				
	National Institute for Breast Cancer Research			$250 pledge			
Educational Opportunity and Support	Literacy Education Fund of Atlanta	$1500	$1,750	$2,000 pledge			
	Highlander Center	$300	$300				
	Ebenezer Baptist Church	$150	$200	$250 pledge			
	Mother's Against Drunk Drivers	$50	$50				
Miscellaneous	St. Paul's Thrift Shop		$750 clothes donation				
	Total Donations	$8,400	$8,500				
	Total Donated Goods / Clothes	$0	$750				

Multi–Year Giving Plan

Area of Funding	Organization	2003	2004	2005	2006	2007	2008
		$	$	$	$	$	$
		$	$	$	$	$	$
		$	$	$	$	$	$
		$	$	$	$	$	$
		$	$	$	$	$	$
		$	$	$	$	$	$
		$	$	$	$	$	$
		$	$	$	$	$	$
		$	$	$	$	$	$
	Total Donations:	$	$	$	$	$	$
	Total Donated Goods/Clothes:	$	$	$	$	$	$

The philanthropic learning curve

Every philanthropist enters the process of giving from a different point. Your approach to giving depends on your enthusiasm and focus, how much time you have, your understanding of the issues that interest you, and your comfort with analyzing information and making decisions. Becoming an inspired philanthropist takes time. Like any new skill or role, it follows its own trajectory, from exciting periods of rapid learning to frustratingly slow plateaus, and times when it all just feels too hard. During the early months, it is particularly helpful to share your experiences with other donors with whom you can commiserate and who can coach and cheer you on.

There does, however, seem to be a progression common to all philanthropists. H. Peter Karoff of The Philanthropic Initiative has dubbed this progression "the philanthropic curve," and has described it as consisting of the following six levels:

Level one: Becoming a donor

A complex combination of influences, which can include personal and religious values, family background, business and social pressures, ego, and heartfelt response to the world around you, motivates you to become a donor. Giving becomes part of your way of life, your position in the community, your yearning to be a good person. Over time, giving becomes less satisfying, requests increase. For the most part, you give small amounts to an ever-growing number of groups.

Level two: Getting organized

You have enough experience as a donor to be able to analyze your giving patterns, decide what really interests you, and which gifts have awarded you the most satisfaction. You begin to develop priorities and criteria for your giving, learn to say no, and make fewer but larger grants.

Level three: Becoming more strategic

Knowing what issues really interest you, you now realize that you don't know enough about them. So you do research: talking to other donors, to experts in the field, reading, consulting with your community foundation, making site visits to organizations addressing those issues. Your giving becomes more focused, the groups you support reflecting your top priorities.

Level four: Focusing on issues and results

At this stage, you become more interested in results and evaluation. It is important that you maximize your giving and increase the possibilities that it will make a difference. Rather than responding to effects, you begin to investigate underlying causes, focusing on building the capacities of the organizations of the most talented and effective nonprofit leaders. You are more proactive, searching out the best people and organizations to support rather than waiting for requests to come to you.

Level five: Leveraging

At this stage, your giving supports the development and funding of programs designed to meet specific programmatic objectives. You enter into collaborations with other donors and participate in public-private partnerships. You have become increasingly knowledgeable about the issues you fund, about what works, about what can really make a difference.

Level six: Harmony and congruence

You experience a satisfying alignment between your most deeply held values and your giving interests. Your philanthropy is one of the most exciting and fulfilling aspects of your life.

One donor, Harriet Barlow, discussed her development as a donor this way:

> I'm learning over the years what I need to stay energized and optimistic as a giver: some of my funding needs to nurture things I can literally see and touch—murals in my neighborhood, community gardens, projects that affect people I know. Some of my money needs to go towards projects shaping the larger political and economic picture, touching the lives of people I will never meet, perhaps taking longer than my lifetime to bear fruit. For instance, during the Mississippi flood disaster in 1994, I didn't give blankets and canned goods, but instead supported projects that would help people rethink how to build on flood plains.

I also need a balance between funding creative start-ups that get my adrenaline going and directing my money to projects I'm confident will bring results. High-risk and low risk—like a good stock portfolio! When I evaluate my giving, I am not judging whether others have done right by me, but rather assessing my own thought process, how I might become more strategic, more deeply attuned to what I need as a giver at this stage in my life.

Strategic and creative ways to leverage your giving

. . . .

Chapter 9

Relationships with groups you support

▪ ▪ ▪

Some donors decide to limit their giving to being a more significant or major donor to just one or two groups. This may give them the chance to have a more substantive role and closer relationships with those organizations. People choose to work more closely with an organization for many reasons, including wanting to work in partnership to create or leverage change, take advantage of leadership opportunities, explore new careers, or create a balance with a job or family. If you would like to consider developing deeper relationships with the groups you support, this chapter will get you thinking about what you want that relationship to be.

The chapter concentrates on becoming more involved with groups to which you give a substantial major gift by establishing clear lines of communication about the nature of your involvement. It also considers the question of loaning money to nonprofits, and offers some suggestions about how to respond to telephone solicitations and door-to-door canvassers in the context of your giving plan.

Effective donor communication

When you invest in the work of a nonprofit, you are not only expressing your interest in helping to address an issue of concern, you are casting a vote of confidence for the organization's senior staff. If the organization is like most, it may be funded at a bare bones level and each of the senior staff members may already be doing the work of two. While it is important that you understand the issues at hand and how the organization is making the most of your donation, the last thing you will want is to dissipate the time of the staff through ad hoc or random requests for information.

Generally, executive directors recommend that the most productive ways for donors to stay abreast of the organization's work are to attend events and read the group's newsletters, e-messages, Web site, annual reports, and other publications. If you are one of many small donors to the organization—providing less than $500 each year—you have a right and obligation to know how your money is being spent, but if these standard forms of communication from the organization will not meet your needs, you should discuss this with the executive director before making your contribution.

If you contribute more than $500 a year to an organization, you will likely be considered a "major donor." (Organizations usually define who is a major donor in relation to their own budgets. For some, a gift of $100 qualifies as a major gift; for other, larger organizations, major donors give a minimum of $1,000 or more.) As a major donor, you will typically be offered the opportunity to interact with senior staff at some point in the year—either in a one-on-one meeting or at an event. These dialogues and events offer you important opportunities to meet key staff, learn about the most interesting challenges and solutions emerging from the organization's work, and ask questions. We recommend that you find time to attend these events for the few organizations or causes you care most about. They provide your best chance to become a more informed and therefore more effective donor.

Development staff in particular are most likely interested and curious to meet you. After all, they are working on cultivating support for the organization or project and you are sharing your enthusiasm for the organization's work. Most fundraisers are excited, albeit sometimes a little nervous, to make personal connections with donors. For both of you the goal of communication is to be better acquainted so that both the relationship and the organization are strengthened. The outcome you should both be seeking is for you to become a better and increasingly generous donor to the organization and a knowledgeable advocate for the agency and cause.

Communicating your support for an organization

Healthy and open communication between key staff and donors can literally make or break an organization. While it is true that as a donor you will be valued for your financial contributions, don't underestimate the great potential value of contributing and communicating your knowledge, contacts, and insights as well. When thinking about how you can add value to your support, consider the following questions about what you might ask executive directors, development directors, and key program staff when you have the opportunity to meet with them, then add two or three of your own.

- In what areas can I, as a donor, be of greater service to the organization?

- Would a challenge grant from me allow you to leverage my contribution to the organization by prompting others to act?

- What are the key issues the organization is focusing on this year? If I know someone with expertise in these areas may I put them in touch with the staff or a board member?

- Are there ways I might contribute my expertise to the organization? (Skills that most nonprofits need include accounting, networking, fundraising, and marketing.)

- What are some of the directions you may be going based on your strategic planning or leadership discussions?

- Are there specific needs that you have now that you'd like to brainstorm with me about?

If you are a major donor, it also makes sense for you to initiate communication with the executive director or other development staff. In fact, if you and the staff person agree on it, it can be especially productive for you to invite a small group of your friends who might be interested in supporting the organization to a meeting with organization staff. A small networking meeting of this nature provides a desirable forum for the director to speak of cutting-edge issues and allows you to be an advocate on behalf of the work you support.

Advice from a development director

Here is some advice to donors from Dana Gillette, Development Director at the Peace Development Fund:

Be honest. Let organizations know about your interests and your willingness to support them. If someone contacts you to see about meeting or about supporting a cause, respond. Whether you say yes or, "Maybe next time, I'm interested, but not available right now," or, "I'm interested in your cause, but not in meeting," or, "No, I'm not interested," your clarity helps.

Let organizations know what you need. If you only want to receive written materials, say so. Being respectful is a two-way street. You deserve to be respected as a donor. So do the staff or volunteers who are moving valuable work forward. Understand your power as a donor and use it wisely.

Recognize that you have a different perspective from organizational staff and board members. Take time to provide feedback. If you see something encouraging that they are doing, let them know. If you are withdrawing support because of something you see happening in the organization, name it. I can't say enough about the occasional e-mails I receive saying, "Keep up the good work," or, "What a great newsletter."

In terms of planning your giving, find some good groups that you want to support and stick with them. If you are just getting to know a group, you may want to start out with a smaller gift and see how it is received. Increase your support over time. A steady donor is an incredible asset.

Communicating donor intent

If you intend to give an organization $500 or more a year, we suggest that you tell them in advance of your gift. It helps development staff and directors of nonprofits with their planning and evaluation to know when a gift will be coming. Likewise, if you're certain that you will no longer be supporting a particular organization, a short note, e-mail, or phone call early in the year will save them from spending the resources to gain or regain your support (see Appendix C, Sample Letters). Healthy transitions from organizations are as important as they are in any relationship.

Even more important than letting a group know that you won't be continuing your gift is to say why, especially if you've become discontent with the organization or don't agree with their direction. "This kind of honest feedback is so rare for most directors to get and it is so useful for us," said a long-time nonprofit leader. Staff are usually eager to hear how their work is perceived; to review decisions that community members, including donors, don't agree with; and to clarify misunderstandings.

Further, for an organization you plan to stop giving to, you may want to work with them to help fill the gap. Consider reviewing the following questions with the development director:

- How can I help you make a healthy transition away from the support I have been providing?

- Could I allocate a percentage of my last donation to the organization to be used for additional fundraising so that you can identify a donor(s) to replace me?

- Are there any introductions I can make for you to help you when I am no longer contributing to the organization?

- Are there ways I might contribute my expertise to the organization (for example, accounting, networking, marketing)?

Giving anonymously

There are reasons not to give anonymously, including wanting acknowledgment for your ideas, contributions, or work on behalf of an organization or wanting to challenge other donors to put their voices and know-how where their money is. Sometimes you want people to know who you are so you can share information and leverage projects. At other times giving anonymously can simplify life and be a practice in humility. Regardless of the size of a gift, you may not want to be recognized as a donor among people you know or work with. Whether you choose to give anonymously is really about your own style and preference.

One situation that can arise is being a major donor while working within an organization as a staff or board member. If you don't want your role as a worker to be affected by your status as a major donor, you have a couple of options. The first is to tell the development director or executive director that you would like to keep your donations private. Explain why it's important to you and get her or him to agree to respect your anonymity and note it in your donor record.

A second option is to make your major gift with a cashier's check or have it come from an unidentified donor-advised fund you have set up at a foundation or financial services company. Shielded by the institution, you're free to ask for reports or for the foundation to conduct an evaluation of your grant or gift (see Donor-Advised Funds in Chapter Ten).

An anonymous gift can have greater impact if it comes with a message. Instead of giving instructions that your gift simply be listed as anonymous to the public, consider substituting descriptions such as "from a young change agent," or "from a dedicated environmentalist," or "from a concerned, gay activist."

One person who was volunteering for an organization to which he also was a major donor said that volunteering gave him insights into the work of the group that no proposal could ever communicate. The one person on staff who knew about his giving respected his privacy, so he could check out the work quietly, help a project he cared deeply about, and know how well the money was being used. While he had to deal with the internal split of being covert in his donor role, he felt it was the best way he could maintain his boundaries and do some real good.

Loans

Occasionally an organization faces a time-limited cash-flow bind and a short-term loan could help them get back to financial self-sufficiency. This is often true of start-up organizations or projects, or when priorities of major funders change and an organization is left without an expected source of income. Enormous swings in the economy such as those of the first years of the twenty-first century also have left some organizations with cash reserves depleted. Some money to tide them over while they gear up other fundraising activities may be crucial.

If you've been a steady and major donor to an organization, the time might come when the organization approaches you for a loan. If you've had a close relationship with the organization, their financial situation should not come as a surprise to you. If you're particularly close to the group, however, your emotional connection might make it more difficult to assess the practicality of their request.

If you do consider loaning money to an organization, we urge you to get financial and legal advice and to have a formal loan agreement signed and dated and a reasonable repayment schedule established. Add a clause for mediation or arbitration should the loan need to be renegotiated, and be sure to send loan payment reminders and pre-addressed payment envelopes sixty and thirty days before each payment is due.

Worksheet 9.1 presents the questions that might help you decide whether making a loan would be a good move. (Appendix E addresses issues that arise concerning loaning money to friends.)

Setting boundaries: How to handle requests

Most people are not receptive when people come to their door for money. They can't stand phone calls from groups they know nothing about and even get cranky about calls from groups they love. They often don't want to go to lunches for donors, don't have the time to attend every event, and hate direct mail.

If you, too, dislike these unwanted incursions into your life, the key is to choose to engage with the kind of fundraising that best informs and inspires you and set limits on the rest. Here are some suggested responses that may help you establish your boundaries with requests for donations you do not wish to make.

When someone comes to your door

I'm sorry. I respect that you're trying to make a living and care about XYZ group. But I don't make gifts in this manner. If you want to leave me material, with your name on the envelope as the solicitor, I will be happy to consider it, and will call the group to check it out. If I send a contribution, I will use your envelope. Thank you.

or

I don't make gifts in this way. It's nothing personal. Good luck.

Loan Analysis

1. **Outline the practical aspects of the loan request:**

   Amount: $_____

   Time period: _____

   Interest bearing? _____ Yes _____ No. If yes, percent? _____

   Purpose: _____

   _____

   _____

   Is the amount reasonable for the need? _____ Yes _____ No.

   Will there be a formal contract? _____ Yes _____ No.

   Will there be a provision for extension? _____ Yes _____ No.

   Is there a possibility of default? _____ Yes _____ No.

   What will be used as collateral? _____

   _____

   _____

2. **Decide on your contingency provisions:**

   If there is difficulty with repayment will I want to have mediation? If so, will it be paid for equally or by the organization? _____

   _____

   Will I accept a trade in lieu of cash repayment? If so, what?

   _____

   _____

   _____

   _____

3. Answer the following questions about the organization:

a. Who's asking, and do I respect and trust them?

_____

_____

b. What is the opinion of community or leadership sources?

_____

_____

c. Does the organization have a solid financial track record?

_____

_____

d. Is this a crisis or temporary transition? If it is a crisis, is this a pattern and can the loan help to change that?

_____

_____

e. Where will the funds for repayment come from?

_____

_____

f. How healthy does the agency seem to me?

1	2	3	4	5
Thriving				Brink of disaster

What will the impact of my loan be at this time?

_____

_____

_____

_____

4. Answer the following questions for yourself:

Am I willing to help with additional fundraising? _____ Yes _____ No.

Is there other information that I need in order to consider making a loan at a level that is appropriate and comfortable?

_____

_____

If I make the loan, do I want to be anonymous? _____ Yes _____ No.

If I do not want to be anonymous, do I want recognition? If yes, what?

_____

_____

_____

_____

_____

_____

_____

_____

_____

_____

_____

_____

_____

_____

_____

_____

_____

When someone calls from a group you don't know or care about

I'm sorry, but I don't give money over the phone. Good luck.

or

What you're doing is wonderful work, I'm sure, but I don't give in this manner. Send me some information by mail and I'll consider it.

Other possible responses:

I've already allocated my budget for this year.
I'm giving to groups that are particularly important to me.
I'm concentrating my available funds on other issues this year.

For groups you give money or time to

Please contact me only _____ times a year. I would prefer to hear from you and receive information about the organization _____ (by phone, mail, personal visit).
Please do not pass my name on to any other organizations.

or

I'm interested in what's happening in this area; please keep me informed about other organizations doing complementary work or events, demonstrations, or actions I might take.

When groups send you mail you don't want

Here's one donor's approach:

I put all requests that I don't care about in one box, and ones I do care about in another. Once a year, I write to all the ones I don't care about and ask them to remove me from their mailing list. Sometimes groups buy magazine mailing lists that I may be on unbeknownst to them, so I may occasionally hear from them after all. But I feel I have done my part to try to reduce my mail and save them expenses too.

Donor bill of rights

A consortium of agencies concerned about the field of philanthropy developed the following "Donor Bill of Rights" as an underpinning for building trust between donors and nonprofit organizations.

Philanthropy is based on voluntary action for the common good. It is a tradition of giving and sharing that is primary to the quality of life. To assure that philanthropy merits the respect and trust of the general public, and that donors and prospective donors can have full confidence in the not-for-profit organizations and causes they are asked to support, we declare that all donors have these rights:

i To be informed of the organization's mission, of the way the organization intends to use donated resources, and of its capacity to use donations effectively for their intended purposes.

ii To be informed of the identity of those serving on the organization's governing board and to expect the board to exercise prudent judgment in its stewardship responsibilities.

iii To have access to the organization's most recent financial statements.

iv To be assured their gifts will be used for the purposes for which they are given.

v To receive appropriate acknowledgment and recognition.

vi To be assured that information about their donations is handled with respect and with confidentiality to the extent provided by law.

vii To expect that all relationships with individuals representing organizations of interest to the donor will be professional in nature.

viii To be informed whether those seeking donations are volunteers, employees of the organization or hired solicitors.

ix To have the opportunity for their names to be deleted from mailing lists that an organization may intend to share.

x To feel free to ask questions when making a donation and to receive prompt, truthful and forthright answers.

Developed by American Association of Fund Raising Counsel (AAFRC), Association for Healthcare Philanthropy (AHP), Council for Advancement and Support of Education (CASE), Association of Fundraising Professionals (AFP)

Inspired philanthropists . . .

- Create a giving plan and budget and give throughout the year
- Have a vision of the effect they want to have
- Do their homework and see and meet leaders and groups
- Align their giving, investing, and volunteering with their values.
- Evaluate agencies and leaders they intend to invest in
- Increase their giving annually as inflation adds to the cost of nonprofits' work
- Look for models and solutions beyond and within their local community
- Stay committed as donors for more than three years
- Never leave home without their address books
- Mentor other donors
- Work for lasting change by seeking the root causes of poverty and other social ills
- Seek transformative, system-shifting solutions
- Give both first and last in funding campaigns
- Communicate well and are responsive to requests
- Are respectful of staff and volunteer members' time
- Are sensitive about the inherent power differential they have as donors
- Give before they are asked
- Have conscious closures with organizations
- Open doors and encourage new partnerships
- Bring other funders to the table
- Offer their time and expertise as well as money
- Offer their leadership on committees and boards
- Ask for money on behalf of organizations and leaders they support
- Ask what is needed from leaders and practitioners who may be more involved than they are

Chapter 10

The many ways to give

▪ ▪ ▪

There are many structures you can use as vehicles for your giving. Some, such as bequests and donor-advised funds, have been around for quite a while. Others discussed in this chapter have grown out of new strategies for giving, new methods of donor involvement and education, new structures for decision-making, and new decision makers.

In this chapter we present brief descriptions of some of these structures and vehicles and go into more depth on some of the newer ones. You will probably want to learn a lot more about any of the ways that sound interesting to you. Increasingly, associations of nonprofits or community foundations are offering seminars on ways to give and financial planning for donors.

All of the giving models discussed here apply to any giving budget. While donor-advised funds, venture philanthropy, and donor circles involve check writing of usually more than $5,000, many people take advantage of these forms by pooling donations. For any form of giving, clarifying values, defining a vision, and creating a giving plan are the building blocks on which to base your actions.

Common vehicles for giving

Bequests: Leaving a stated sum of money or a percentage outright to nonprofits, family, and/or friends by naming them in your will. You can also structure a trust that will benefit charitable organizations or individuals during or after your lifetime.

Community Development Financial Institution (CDFI): A lending institution (including community loan funds, community banks, and credit unions) whose mission is to reinvest in targeted, underserved communities. CDFIs are supported by institutions and individual investors and donors who preserve capital while these lending agencies make that capital accessible to a community of organizations and individuals.

Community Foundation: A public foundation that receives donations from a broad: base and whose charter is to serve its community or issue-specific population. There are nearly 1,000 Community Foundations all over the United States and a growing number internationally. Community foundations vary in age, asset base, level of service to donors, politics, and level of community involvement.

Corporate Foundation: A private foundation established by a business corporation as a means of carrying out systemic programs of charitable giving. The board of directors is usually composed of senior executives and directors of the company; in most cases funds are received and distributed each year from current profits of the parent company.

Donor Circle/Giving Circle: Types of pooled funds. Donors make a one- to five-year commitment to study, donate funds, and become advocates around a specific issue, region, or population.

Donor-Advised Fund: A fund established by an individual donor or group of donors at an existing community foundation, public foundation, or federation, or through a philanthropic program at a financial services institution. Donors make recommendations about where they would like their contributions to go; the fund handles the administrative details, IRS reporting, and investment management for a defined fee.

E-Philanthropy: Online nonprofit and philanthropic activity. This can include Web-based giving, volunteering, advocacy, and organizing.

Family Foundation: A private foundation involving family and extended family and sometimes community advisors.

Life Insurance and Retirement Assets: Nonprofits or individuals can be named as charitable beneficiaries of at least a percentage of these retirement and contingency investment assets. Financial and insurance advisors are familiar with how to do this.

Pooled Fund: Many individuals pooling any amount of money together to gain philanthropic leverage. Friends, service clubs, graduation classes and, most recently, a proliferation of giving clubs have created pooled giving funds.

Private Foundation: An organization whose function is to give away money; supported by a small number of private donations.

Supporting Foundation: Also known as a Supporting Organization. A tax-exempt organization, usually with at least $1 million in assets, that has reduced limitations on charitable deductions.

Trusts: A variety of vehicles that can offer lifetime income and/or tax advantages to you, your family, or favorite charity. Planned giving specialists and attorneys are knowledgeable about the various forms of trusts (which include charitable remainder trusts, charitable lead trusts, qualified terminable interest property, life estates, unitrusts, annuity trusts, uniform credit trusts, generation skipping trusts, and qualified personal residence trusts).

Venture Philanthropy: The application of the investment and management practices of venture capitalism to philanthropic giving.

Ways to give: Each serving different needs

Your giving will be more effective if you're specific about the ways you can give your time, talents, and treasures; if you're clear about your decision-making process; and if you specify which, if any, of your giving will be part of a formal group or grantmaking entity. Exercise 10.1 is designed to help you think about the different ways there are to give and which of them are right for you.

Giving Methods

5–10 minutes

Put a check mark in the appropriate column for each of the methods you've used or ways you could consider giving financial support.

	I have used this method	I want information on this method	Not applicable to me or not interested
Financial gifts			
Written a check	___	___	___
Given cash	___	___	___
Donated by credit card	___	___	___
Given stock	___	___	___
Given real estate or other holdings	___	___	___
Charitable estate planning	___	___	___
Designated insurance policies or IRAs to a nonprofit beneficiary	___	___	___
Other: _____	___	___	___
Other: _____	___	___	___
Non-financial gifts			
Given house or space for fundraising events, activists' or artists' retreats, or issues briefings	___	___	___
Written a letter or placed a phone call of recommendation (leverage)	___	___	___
Given equipment	___	___	___
Given skills	___	___	___
Other: _____	___	___	___
Other: _____	___	___	___

	I have used this method	I want information on this method	Not applicable to me or not interested
Decision making			
By self	____	____	____
With partner	____	____	____
With family (multi ages)	____	____	____
With groups of other people from similar incomes	____	____	____
With mixed-income group	____	____	____
With group of co-workers or friends	____	____	____
Gave decision-making power to others	____	____	____
To group of professionals in the field, or representatives of constituency groups or activists	____	____	____
To a staff member, program advisor	____	____	____
To someone else to decide	____	____	____
Other: _____	____	____	____
Other: _____	____	____	____
Mechanism			
Public community foundation or federation	____	____	____
Donor-advised fund	____	____	____
Donor circle	____	____	____
Giving circle	____	____	____
Online donation	____	____	____
Venture philanthropic fund	____	____	____
Loan to a nonprofit or individual	____	____	____
Investment in a community loan or micro-enterprise fund	____	____	____
As part of a mixed group of low-income and wealthy activists	____	____	____

	I have used this method	I want information on this method	Not applicable to me or not interested
Workplace or payroll deduction	_____	_____	_____
Family foundation	_____	_____	_____
Supporting foundation	_____	_____	_____
Other: _____	_____	_____	_____
Other: _____	_____	_____	_____

Designation of donations

Operating expenses	_____	_____	_____
Capital expenses (e.g., building or equipment)	_____	_____	_____
Grantmaking funds	_____	_____	_____
Leadership sabbaticals	_____	_____	_____
Endowment gifts	_____	_____	_____
Matching or challenge gifts	_____	_____	_____
Technical assistance	_____	_____	_____
Scholarships	_____	_____	_____
Loans	_____	_____	_____
Existing debt reduction	_____	_____	_____

Time frame

One-year gift	_____	_____	_____
Multi-year gift	_____	_____	_____
Gift with no amount of time attached	_____	_____	_____
Planned gift (during lifetime or upon death)	_____	_____	_____

Reflection:

1. What is your analysis of your methods of giving?

_____

_____

_____

_____

2. What methods do you want to learn more about?

_____

_____

_____

_____

3. What information do you need and who or what resource can best answer your questions?

_____

_____

_____

_____

_____

_____

_____

_____

_____

_____

_____

_____

_____

Some frequently used ways to give

This section goes into more detail about some frequently used ways to give.

Donor-advised funds

Donor-advised funds offer an alternative to establishing your own private foundation. These giving vehicles have been available through public foundations and the United Way for many years. In the last five years companies that provide financial services, such as Fidelity, Vanguard, Schwab, and American Express, have also established donor-advised charitable giving programs. The amount of money that has been donated through donor-advised funds in the past decade represents a huge area of growth in American philanthropy.

A donor-advised fund enables a donor to make an outright, irrevocable contribution of cash or securities to an organization that acts as fiscal manager of the fund and distributes the fund's income or assets to nonprofit organizations. Typically, a minimum of $5,000 to $10,000 is required to open a donor-advised account. Individuals, families, groups, and corporations can establish a donor-advised fund. The donor or donors may make periodic recommendations to the board or directors or overseers of the donor's account regarding distribution of the fund's income, but these recommendations are not legally binding. In theory, this means that a donor relinquishes ultimate authority over their fund in return for the convenience, tax deductions, and potential cost savings of having a larger institution manage their charitable contributions. In practice, however, such institutions rely substantially on donor input on how the funds are distributed.

Among the most commonly marketed benefits of donor-advised funds are the following:

- They are easy to establish.
- Administration of the fund is handled by the parent organization.
- A charitable deduction can be taken as soon as the donation to the fund is made even if the funds distributions take place over several years. Thus, mak-

ing a single gift to a donor-advised fund can provide a well-timed charitable tax deduction without rushing major gift decisions.

- Currently, no capital gains tax is imposed on long-term appreciated securities donated to these funds.

- Costs to manage the funds are low; annual fees total approximately 1–7 percent of each fund's principal, which includes investment fees as well as the fee for basic administration of grants. Many community foundations have grant-making staff who also can be contracted for special or expanded research, due diligence, or evaluation.

- The fund balance grows from both additional gifts and investment earnings and growth.

- Because an institution is managing the fund, it can carry on donors' charitable values beyond their lifetimes.

- Financial and programmatic reports are informative and easy to read; some on-line services and private exchange forums especially for donors provide added value.

- Donor education programs or site visits are sometimes provided for fund holders, especially through community foundations.

- Where the granting areas are in alignment with their missions, public foundations (such as women's funds and some other community-based foundations) also handle limited numbers of donor-advised funds.

If you decide to be an anonymous donor through a donor-advised fund vehicle, you may also want to make a small donation outside of the fund ($100–$250) to your highest-funded projects. That way, you can get direct information about the progress of the organizations and leaders you care about. Another way to keep informed about those projects is to ask your donor-advised staff to share with you the files that they may have collected, as well as annual reports, other information, and evaluations of the agencies before you consider repeat funding. You might also consider making a gift to the general fund of the community foundation or to special initiatives.

When thinking about setting up a donor-advised fund, be aware of the following potential challenges and think about how you will handle them:

- In most philanthropic or donor-advised accounts established in financial service institutions the funds are typically managed in much the same way as financial accounts, with the emphasis on administration and distribution rather than on donor engagement and education.

- The staff of the community foundation or financial services institution holding your donor-advised assets may not have expertise in the interest area you choose to give to, or may not know the current status of a specific group you have heard about or previously given to, so it may be difficult to get sound advice.

- There is no legal requirement for the institution to move your income or grants into the community. Moreover, the financial services institution or community foundation that manages your funds often benefit from fees acquired based on assets held. Therefore, the burden of responsibility for making sure your money keeps moving into the nonprofit world is on you.

- At some financial institutions or community foundations, a single staff person may manage hundreds of donor-advised funds. Before you place your money, learn what level of research and engagement are available for your account or what additional services you may purchase. Be sure the person you collaborate with has program and community experience in your area of interest, not simply philanthropic administrative experience.

- If you choose to hire an outside philanthropic advisor or researcher, the financial services institution or community foundation managing your fund may not have experience in working in such a team. Ask if they do and what the fiduciary and management needs will be. Some institutions are able to offer such team efforts only to larger fund holders (donors giving away $100,000 or more a year).

- The entity managing your funds may not allow you to give nationally or globally.

- You may need to work with staff at the organization holding your account to obtain donor education from community leaders. Find out if they are open to your ideas for programs. You might help them by funding such donor education programs as a benefit to other donors.

Family foundations

Of approximately 55,000 foundations in the United States, about 35,000 are family foundations. The fact that the number of family foundations doubled in the past twenty years reflects not only tax changes that encouraged the formation of foundations or donor-advised funds, but also families' strong desires to use the form of a foundation as a tool to bring families closer together. (Families with less than $100,000 to give annually or with less than $2 million in assets may not want to set up a formal foundation. Instead, they can create a donor-advised fund at their local community foundation as described above.)

What begins for many heads of family as a desire to shelter family-held or earned resources from taxes can evolve into a creative way for families to get to know each other better and work together for the public good. In some instances, of course, it can also perpetuate feelings of isolation, domination, or neglect among family members.

Advisors and consultants to family foundations have become a new industry. Organizations such as the National Center on Family Philanthropy, the Council on Foundations' Family Foundation program, and More than Money provide advice, referrals, publications, and conferences. Wealth advisors, philanthropic consultants, and community foundation staff are skilled at helping families find the best resources to create healthy family dialogue and decision-making processes. They can help family members sort out their values and interest areas and come to some guiding principles and processes that can make family and community interactions valuable and respectful to all.

If you are considering starting a family foundation, we urge you to hire a consultant early in the process. Just a few hours and a few thousand dollars of an established and experienced consultant's time can save your family months of difficult decision making. Even better is to work with a philanthropic consultant over several years to help improve the confidence and relationships within your family, disentangle old habits of interacting, and create new and creative ways of making your family foundation a positive experience.

To begin, families can use our sample values and interest lists to share their personal (and then collective) values and goals (see Exercise 2.3 in Chapter Two). Families that have begun to discuss giving and volunteering together are often surprised by all they learn. For example, a man learned that the sister he thought he had nothing in common with was a donor to one of the organizations he cherished the most. So often we are filled with assumptions from childhood about our siblings and parents. Meanwhile, some of them have become skilled or insightful people! Creating dialogues, e-mail exchanges, family foundations, or family giving funds together can provide new ways of relating and can even help heal past differences.

If you determine that you and your family will have your own family foundation, we emphasize the benefits of including outside or community representatives on your board or decision-making bodies. These members will not only add balance and sometimes peacemaking to family differences, but can be sources of outside wisdom or mentoring for family members.

As with any giving, family giving must deal with a number of questions: "Should we give anonymously?" "When should we give, how, how much, and to whom?" "In what geographic region shall we give?" "How can we make decisions when we have so many different priorities?"

In addition, the question of whether next-generation donors should always defer to the interests of the older, sometimes founding generation of the foundation often arises. While it is natural that a family will want to honor the foundation's founder with gifts to some of his or her favorite charities, the older generation should also consider sparking the next generation's own creativity in giving by decision-making power over some meaningful amount of the money to be given away. For example, one-half could be designated to go to the long-time interests of the founder(s), while the other half is allocated to the next generation to fund their own interests. Or, one-fourth of a foundation's outlay could be earmarked for innovative projects or for core operating support of tried-and-true nonprofits the family might want to fund jointly.

Establishing committees that provide for intergenerational leadership and mentoring provides a wonderful learning opportunity. This way the next generation can offer their ideas and concerns about everything from the grants process to the investment policies.

We also recommend giving the next generation time to meet separately and to have their own support, perhaps from a consultant they choose to work with or from contemporaries of another, more experienced family foundation. Expanding the next generation's expertise, leadership, and voices are key steps to making the current intergenerational transfer of wealth successful. Foundations for Change and Resource Generation are valuable organizational resources for the younger generation.

Our final three recommendations in this section cover staffing, site visits, and budgets.

The Council on Foundations estimates that only 5 percent of foundations have paid professional staff. The remaining 95 percent are run by family members or volunteers. Staffing your own foundation is a lot of work, yet can be extremely rewarding. There are a wealth of resources and models available that can greatly ease the process and are worth pursuing (see Resources).

Visits to projects you are interested in are also invaluable. A very small percentage of foundations make site visits to nonprofits they fund or are considering funding. However, much education and community-building occurs in these visits, so we urge you to encourage the volunteer leadership of your family to ensure that these kinds of opportunities are available.

Finally, as you develop a budget for your foundation each year, provide for key learning opportunities. These can include representatives coming to inform you about current issues in foundation giving, or family members attending national, regional, or local issue-specific or industry-related conferences or site visits.

DEVELOPING A "STATEMENT OF DONOR LEGACY" A statement that sets forth the legacy that founding donors wish to leave can be an invaluable tool for a family foundation, as it provides important background information about the foundation's mission for present and future trustees.

Inevitably family foundations move from being solely directed by the original donor to having decisions made by a board with multiple generations of the original donor's family and sometimes the involvement of non-family members. In this situation, a donor legacy statement can ease any doubts or anxieties family members might have about giving away the donor's wealth or assuming responsibility for more of the foundation's grantmaking—or even about continuing the foundation after the life of the founding donor or donors. Such a statement describes the donor's vision and intent in setting up the foundation and touches on the history of the foundation's giving to date. In doing so, it effectively takes some areas of decision making off the table, reducing opportunities for family discord or contention. A donor legacy statement is also an invaluable guide to the donor's wishes for the time when they will no longer be available for consultation.

Founding donors and board members are involved in creating this document. The donors must clarify the family values they want to continue in the decision making of future generations and how much latitude they want to give future generations to exercise judgment that might substantially transform the nature of the foundation's giving. The donors should also address their grantmaking concerns and wishes regarding current funding obligations. Where a board already exists, board members should think about questions that might arise about future giving of the foundation and their individual preferences about its operation.

As a statement of donor legacy made by the family foundation, the document should be formally approved by the board. If a family is creating a donor intent statement when the original donors can no longer be consulted, the process must rely more on detective work and recalled anecdotal information. Some families choose to enlist the help of an outside philanthropic consulting firm, professional writer, or videographer for their expertise and objectivity in conceiving this document.

Estate planning and charitable giving

Estate planning means planning for the orderly handling, disposition, and administration of your goods and money when you die. Charitable estate planning is a vehicle that can help you give after you die in ways and amounts that you could not during your lifetime.

There is a misconception that only those with a lot of money or other assets need to undertake thoughtful estate planning, including writing a will. That's not true. If you have any money in a bank or retirement account, own a home or other real estate, or own anything of any value—a car, a work of art, jewelry—you need to decide what will happen to these things after your death. If you don't decide, the government will, and anyone you hoped would benefit will lose to taxes much of what they would have received. Estate planning, in short, lets you provide for loved ones, make gifts to causes you care about, and save your heirs income and estate taxes.

To understand estate planning, you need to understand capital gains. Capital gains are the difference between an asset's purchase price and its selling price when the difference is positive. If, when you die, non-income-producing assets such as homes, land, and artwork that you may have owned for years or decades have increased in value over that time, the increase is considered a capital gain. According to the group Leave a Legacy, these gains can be taxed at up to 80 percent if those assets are not held in some sort of trust.

The Nonprofit Times estimates that more than 70 percent of U.S. households nationwide contribute to charity each year. However, only 5.7 percent of households surveyed by the National Council on Planned Giving in 1992 had planned a charitable bequest. In 1996, of 79,346 estate tax forms filed with the federal government for estates in excess of $600,000, only 18 percent listed a charitable gift. That means that 82 percent of the nation's wealthiest individuals left nothing to charity.

In response to the need for more education about bequests, a national program called Leave A Legacy offers free education programs to nonprofits and their boards and donors on the legal, financial, and planning aspects of legacy gifts. We urge you to attend at least two such programs, because it can take several hours to fully comprehend and consider the many options for simple or complex estate or planned gifts. If you'd like to start thinking about planning for your estate on your own, here are five simple steps to consider:

1. ***Identify your goals.*** These could include protecting assets for your beneficiaries, perpetuating a family legacy, making charitable gifts, minimizing taxes, and providing for family members.

2. ***Identify your beneficiaries.*** As Miven Booth Trageser did (see Chapter One), spend some thoughtful time planning where and to whom you want to make these gifts. The giving plan you devised in Chapter Seven may serve as a road map.

3. ***Identify your assets.*** List and calculate all your assets, including cash, appreciated securities, appreciated property, tangible personal property (for example, cars, jewelry, works of art), retirement accounts, and life insurance.

4. ***Determine your liquidity needs.*** Determine the amount of money you need to live on now and project possible major expenses in the future, including enough money to cover expenses in case of an emergency.

5. ***Create, implement, and monitor a plan.*** For many people this is a fun and empowering experience. You can write up your own will, using some of the references you'll find in Resources. If your estate is complicated, estate lawyers, tax accountants, legacy consultants, and financial planners can all help you design exactly what you want. Your estate may also benefit from many useful insurance products that can provide for your tax responsibilities or expand your gifts to beneficiaries.

Each of us can leave a legacy. Begin today to consider what difference you want to make and then be sure to complete the documents, if only a handwritten will. Groups and leaders you care about count on this aspect of your leadership.

Charitable estate planning

The portion of an estate plan that includes charitable gifts can take many forms and offers many creative alternatives benefiting both non-charitable donors and charitable recipients. For example, charitable estate planning vehicles such as charitable remainder trusts can allow you to transfer highly appreciated assets to a charity and still receive an income stream from those assets while you're alive. When you do this, you bypass capital gains taxes and take an income-tax deduction. Or, with a charitable lead trust, for example, you can designate a nonprofit as the current beneficiary of some assets (that organization receives the income) and your children as the remainder beneficiaries, so they will receive the assets following a specific period of time.

Charitable estate planning is a complex, creative, and highly technical field that a competent estate lawyer and certified public accountant can help you with. Many people, especially those with sizable assets, find that lawyers and tax accountants do not take the initiative to suggest charitable estate planning options. You don't need to become an expert yourself, but you do need to ask your financial advisors about charitable trust planning vehicles that will allow you to pursue your charitable goals and enable you and your heirs to save substantially on taxes. Your local university, hospital, public or community foundation, or any other large nonprofit institution cultivating donors probably offers charitable estate planning workshops.

If you decide that you want to leave money or a valuable gift to a charity or nonprofit organization, one question to consider is whether you should let the organization know that they have been named as a beneficiary in your will or trust. While knowing they will someday receive a bequest from you is important for an organization, it may also lead to preferential treatment. If you fear that such knowledge will encourage the organization to ask you for more money during your lifetime or to treat you differently than they might now, communicate your preference around such things when telling them about the bequest.

It is very important that your will be as specific as possible in a letter or more formal document or on tape so that those executing your estate understand your charitable intent. Giving specific designations or examples of what kinds of projects or geographic limitations you have in mind for your charitable bequests is an important part of your estate planning.

One avenue to ensuring your bequests are handled as you would wish is to designate one or more people to be charitable advisors after your death. These may be family members, friends, philanthropic or community leaders, or financial or legal professionals who have known you or your interests well. These advisors interpret your wishes with a nonprofit you may have named in a bequest or with a

Statement of donor legacy

▪ ▪ ▪ ▪ ▪ ▪ ▪ ▪ ▪ ▪ ▪ ▪ ▪ ▪ ▪ ▪ ▪

The following statement was created with the help of the consulting firm Grants Management Associates (see Resources) and adopted by the foundation board in 1997, one year before Sidney Stoneman, who, along with his wife, was the original donor, passed away.

In 1957 we established this foundation in memory and honor of Sidney's parents. Over the years, it has served as a vehicle for our charitable giving.

When the foundation was established, its legal instrument made no specifications about the geographic reach of the foundation's giving, the composition of its board, or any kind of focus for its charitable contributions. For many years, the foundation operated informally, with funding decisions initiated primarily by Sidney and with little public visibility.

In 1990 we decided to involve our extended family in the foundation, and formalized the decision by hiring Grants Management Associates to assist with the development of guidelines and the establishment of grantmaking processes. We developed an eight-person board, including three non-family members, and published guidelines that describe a grantmaking process for the foundation and a geographic scope.

As the foundation moves into the future, at some point it will do so without our involvement. When we pass on, the foundation will become larger and will represent a greater responsibility as well as a greater opportunity. We have every confidence that our wonderful family will provide the thoughtful guidance required along the way.

As the foundation's donors, we would like to think that the foundation will always be rooted in the values and traditions of our family. The purpose of this document is to convey this wish to current and future members of the board of directors.

Part of the Stoneman family's identity and interests have been in the Jewish community. Our participation in this community has been an acknowledgement of our own roots and has never promoted sectarianism. Rather, it has supported the achievement of excellence among Jewish people and the fostering of a spirit of brotherhood and inclusiveness with all peoples. We would like our family foundation to acknowledge and continue this participation in the Jewish community in the future.

While we have been significant contributors to specific Jewish organizations over the years, we do not want to specify the recipients of future foundation support in this area. Nor do we wish to suggest that a certain amount or portion of available grant funds be directed to these organizations. We ask simply that some funds be directed to Jewish organizations, in recognition of the family's history and values that have been part of the Jewish community in this country and beyond.

Second, the Stoneman family has its roots in Boston. Generations of the family made their homes here, starting with Sidney's father, who emigrated from Russia. Boston has been our home too and here is the community of friends and associates that have meant the most to us. We would like the Stoneman Family Foundation to continue to have a Boston presence, with a preference but not a requirement that the foundation annually allocate a significant portion of its grants funds to organizations in the Boston area. At the same time, we understand and expect that the balance of the grant funds will be used to support organizations in the geographic area of interest to family members who are serving as foundation directors.

In relation to contributions in the Boston area, there are a few with which we have had a deep involvement over the years. These include Beth Israel Hospital, the Boston Symphony Orchestra, and Combined Jewish Philanthropies. These organizations have been beneficiaries of significant financial contributions made by both the foundation and us personally. For the future, we request that the foundation directors continue to consider requests from these organizations, and judge them in the light of their relevance to the needs of society and their responsiveness to the purposes of the foundation.

The Stoneman Family Foundation always has been a family affair. We would like this to continue into the future. We feel the best way to ensure continued family involvement is by board membership. It is our hope that Stoneman family members will constitute a majority of the board in perpetuity. Failing that, we would request liquidation of the foundation. This being said, we make no further presumptions about representation of different branches and generations of the family, except to say that we expect that the foundation directors will establish policies relating to board membership that are inclusive and equitable.

Adapted from the Statement of Donor Legacy for the Stoneman Family Foundation in *Living The Legacy,* a journal on donor legacy from the National Center for Family Philanthropy, 2001.

foundation or trust that you may have contributed to or set up upon your death. We suggest you convene this group of advisors or representatives during your lifetime, if only for one meeting, to let them know your dreams and charitable intent. Be sure the meeting has a note taker, or is taped and transcribed for use when needed.

Corporate philanthropy

While large and small businesses are often very generous with contributions of goods or services, as you can see from the chart from *Giving USA* in Chapter One, corporate philanthropy represented only 4.3 percent of all that was contributed financially to the nonprofit sector in 2001. If you are part of a corporation, perhaps as staff or shareholder in a family business, and you want to encourage the corporation to address social objectives in an inspired and planned way, the following are some tips and references for more information and great examples of how corporations can practice inspired philanthropy.

For-profit businesses are directly accountable to different stakeholders than are individuals and families. This means that considerations such as business performance are involved in addressing social concerns. As with developing a personal giving plan, being involved in starting a corporate foundation begins with defining priority interest areas and ways to get involved in these areas. These activities, sometimes called "corporate engagement," form part of an ongoing corporate strategy for community involvement and enhanced business performance. As such, they offer the potential to have a positive impact on low-income communities as well as to have direct or indirect benefit to the corporation. Corporate engagement can include both philanthropic activities and activities that tap into the corporation's core competencies and operations, such as its power to purchase, develop products, invest, market, hire and train, and innovate.

In many cases, the most challenging aspect of corporate philanthropy is persuading others in the company that it is a worthwhile undertaking. Corporate board members, shareholders, and even employees can perceive philanthropy as a drain on scarce resources or as a distraction from the "business of business." A November, 2000 research report, *Conversations with Disbelievers: Persuading Compa-*

nies to Address Social Challenges, brings together much of the available quantitative evidence of the financial benefits that companies can gain by effectively addressing social challenges as a core element of their business strategy. Sponsored by the Ford Foundation and written by John Weiser and Simon Zadek, the report also summarizes three broad sets of drivers that have moved corporate managers to address social objectives:

- **Values:** represents an expression of core company values

- **Strategy:** supports or enhances a key long-term business strategy

- **Pressure:** responds to a short-term external pressure such as regulation or advocacy group activities

Values, strategy, and consideration of community needs are also key components of the Inspired Philanthropy model of creating a giving plan.

One step to starting a corporate foundation or giving program is to convene or survey a representative cross-section of company stakeholders (key executives, employees, board members, and community members) to answer the following questions:

- What is our motivation for creating a philanthropic initiative? Are we interested in doing good or merely looking good?

- What are the values of this corporation? How can our values best be expressed to the world?

- Who are we most interested in benefiting—our employees, our community, our industry, our country, the world?

- How can we best leverage the full range of our resources to provide a win–win outcome for our stakeholders and community?

- Do we have enough philanthropic expertise on our team or do we need outside help?

The answers to these questions will point to the next steps.

For more information on the field of Corporate Philanthropy, you might want to check the following organizations through their Web sites:

The Center for Corporate Citizenship at Boston College—www.bc.edu

Council on Foundations—www.cof.org

Wise Giving—www.wisegiving.org

The Chronicle of Philanthropy—www.philanthropy.com

The Conference Board—www.conference-board.org

CORPORATE PHILANTHROPY IN ACTION Two stories give examples of some corporate philanthropy and the ripple effects it can have.

It's Not Just About Money Mrs. Grossman's, the $25 million-a-year manufacturer of decorative stickers, is the world's largest company of its kind. For years the company had been donating millions of not-quite-perfect stickers to children in hospitals around the world. A few years ago, company employees devised a way to reap a second philanthropic benefit from these castoff stickers. Through the creation of "Mrs. Grossman's Helping Hands," nine- to thirteen-year-olds from one of San Francisco's poorest neighborhoods have been employed to handle packaging and mailing the stickers headed for hospitals. The children in the program are paid one point for every hour they work; the points are redeemable for gift certificates at local department stores.

The program seems to be having a broad effect on the youngsters participating. "We get calls from school principals," explains Mrs. Grossman, "saying, 'Whatever you're doing down there is working. The kids in the program are more social, easier to get along with, aren't picking fights. One of the girls told me that because of the program she is a better friend.'" "It's a win-win-win," observes one philanthropy consultant. "Mrs. Grossman's is a wonderful example of the impact one small program can have on thousands of needy kids."

Corporate Volunteerism The Toronto office of The Boston Consulting Group, self-described as a "strategy consulting group," added a unique incentive for prospective employees. In addition to describing the career opportunities and usual perks of working with a successful international company, BCG makes the point that potential recruits will also have the chance to develop experience as volunteers.

Volunteer opportunities are communicated regularly from management to employees. In addition, at "Community Committee Breakfasts" employees discuss the various charities with which they want to become involved. Moreover, BCG matches employee charitable donations up to preset limits. The result: of the eighty employees at BCG's Toronto office, 70 percent are volunteers.

New strategies in decision making and giving

In the past ten years, the American profile of who makes decisions about donations, what influences those choices, and how donors relate to nonprofits has changed considerably. These changes are reflected in the variety of new ways of giving described in this section.

Giving circles and donor circles: New models of giving

Since the 1990s, giving circles and donor circles have been emerging as new models of giving. Both involve groups of people pooling some philanthropic dollars and making joint decisions on the use of those funds. The difference is in institutional affiliation. Giving circles have no institutional affiliation (except sometimes for fiscal sponsorship). They consist of groups of people with some common interests and values who seek to make philanthropic gifts through collective giving. Donor circles, on the other hand, are programs developed by established giving institutions, often for the benefit of their grantees or their own programs.

GIVING CIRCLES: GRASSROOTS GIVING WITH IMPACT Giving Circles— a kind of social investment club can be a powerful way to create social change and engage in a new frontier in philanthropy. In the Giving Circle model like-minded donors explore and collaborate with one another to make focused social investments with impact. By acting collectively, giving circle members have the chance to infuse the nonprofits of their choice with financial and intellectual capital, resources, and contacts.

A giving circle often begins when an individual brings together a small, informal group of individuals whose members share the following desires:

- To leverage the impact of their charitable contributions with shared expertise and volunteerism

- To connect meaningfully with the communities and causes they care about

- To participate in a social network of people who share similar interests and values

- To learn more about philanthropy as a vehicle for social change

  Among the many advantages of forming giving circles are the following:

- Pooled dollars invested toward a key issue can have a far greater impact than smaller individual gifts

- Collective "know-how" of a group adds value and impact to volunteerism and charitable investments

- Creating partnerships with a smaller number of charities creates a deeper level of involvement and gives a better chance to gauge your return on investment

The number of giving circles is increasing tremendously as they are, above all, a community-building and collaborative learning experience. In a relatively short time, the impact of pooling money and distributing it in one's community can provide enormous satisfaction. It is also fun to participate with and share in learning new information.

Sondra Shaw Hardy's book with The Women's Philanthropy Institute, *Creating a Women's Giving Circle* (see Appendix F, Resources) describes the common elements of giving circles:

- Membership is broad, diverse and inclusive.

- The amounts of money contributed may or may not be the same from each member and are given at least annually. Philanthropy is an activity in which anyone may be involved.

- The money is pooled.

- Members determine how the money will be distributed.

- The money is used to help address specific community or institutional needs.

- There are educational opportunities within the giving circle to learn more about philanthropy and finance.

- The membership is proactive and participatory.

- There is a minimum of donor recognition other than personal thanks.

- Volunteers provide most of the circle support.

An example of a giving circle at the high end is Social Venture Partners, a giving circle founded by Microsoft millionaire Paul Brainard and Scott Oki so that they and other high-technology stock holders could gain skills about giving and community involvement. Profiled here are examples of more "ordinary" people forming giving groups, the Friday Night ShoeBox Group of Berkeley, California and the Boston Women's Tzedakah Collective.

Mila Visser't Hooft: The "Friday Night Shoebox" We started the Friday Night Shoebox in 1998. About twelve people regularly attend, along with some "virtual" members. We have among us librarians, doctors, lawyers, non-profit workers, a physicist, a statistician, a biologist, a hydrologist, a poet, and a priest. We each give what we think we would spend on a night's meal out. The amount we each give into the "shoebox" per meeting is not known to the rest of the group: we want to make sure people are completely equal partners whether they give a burrito's worth or the equivalent of a three-course dinner with wine. The money is held at a donor-advised fund at the local community foundation. This lets our donations be tax deductible. The foundation directs our money as we decide.

Our first year was spent primarily on procedural issues, including what to call ourselves and learning what the group considered important to fund. Two minor schisms naturally evolved within the group: how much to give locally, nationally, and internationally; and which kind of organizations to fund—those that are working to change the system or work on policy versus those working within existing frameworks. These topics have provided us with the chance to have a number of very interesting discussions and develop our decision-making process.

We have given away about $3,000 so far and have about $4,000 available. We don't know yet if we are going to make repeat grants or if our philanthropic interests will change substantially over time, but we're enjoying learning from each other and seeing how much more we can do with our collective contributions than any one of us could have done alone.

Sarah Feinberg: Boston Women's Tzedakah Collective The Boston Area Women's Tzedakah Collective is a group of ten young professional women who work and study in the Boston area. Though we have economic, religious, sexual, and cultural differences, we hold a common belief that we receive a great deal from the community in which we live and want to give back to that community. In giving collectively, we overcome our individual differences, knowing we can contribute more than any of us could individually. Our mission is to bring together women who have limited means but enormous passion to make the world better. We want to uncover and explore our essential values. Our goal is to have an impact on our lives and the lives of others.

Since our level of giving is small, we feel that our impact is greater at the local level; we can see it more easily, and we have the chance to become involved with the organizations we donate to.

Some of the women in the group are in the Boston University MBA program, others work in the nonprofit sector. The first year, we collected $500 and donated it all to a local domestic violence shelter. The second year, we collected and donated $1,200 to the local chapter of Suited for Success.

At the beginning of each giving year, we spent three meetings developing our collective values and becoming informed about issues we were interested in. The first year we chose to focus on domestic violence as an area that could affect each of us. The second year we decided that working on economic justice would challenge us for a few reasons:

• Those of us in business school spent a lot of time talking about how to make a lot of money. We wanted to turn this on its head and focus the conversation on money in a socially productive way.

• We wanted to overcome the classic stereotype that many of us identified with that women are not involved in economic issues. We wanted to push ourselves in an area in which we felt less comfortable.

• We see economic issues as some of the root causes of societal problems and feel we can have a larger impact in this area.

- In our private giving we each support women, children and educational causes. We wanted to do something different as a group.

Our group meets each month for about two hours. There are four official volunteer positions: two co-treasurers, a pre-meeting e-mail person, and a note taker. Everyone has an equal stake and voice within the group. This year, we have each committed to participate in at least two community service projects with one or two other members of the collective.

For the first two years, each person contributed $10 per month to the collection. At the end of the second year, as most of us were graduating and entering the working world, we changed the dues structure to be unlimited, but also anonymous, so that everyone will continue to have an equal voice.

In the first year, since we spent so much time learning about philanthropy and our individual ideas and beliefs, we made our funding decision with little information. In the second year, we created a curriculum to learn about the area we were interested in funding and to get hands-on experience through site visits. One site visit, in groups of no more than three people, was made to each organization we were considering. We made follow-up phone calls to organizations where we lacked sufficient information. Our grantmaking decision felt better since we were basing it on data (budget size, constituent size) and other information (how the organization interacts with the rest of the community, structure of the organization and its compatibility with our mission and goals).

By the time we had to make a decision, we understood each other, we trusted each other, and we were able to communicate in a productive way. We decided fairly quickly that we were interested in funding a smaller organization, one that did not have a large fundraising structure or easy access to resources. Our conversation focused on issues of need, sustainability, and fit with our interests. Ultimately, we created a pros and cons chart for the top three organizations we were considering for a donation.

Each member has her own reasons for joining the Tzedakah Collective, among which are a few themes. Some wanted to meet other women who are committed to giving on a limited income and to be able to make more of a difference than when donating alone. Many wanted a structured way to donate time and money to causes they believe in. Others joined for the social aspect of spending time together each month. The collective gives us a way to think constructively about what issues matter to each of us individually and collectively and a way to learn more about issues in the Boston area that we might otherwise not think about. It enables us to take the time to research the best place for our money, which we don't have the time to do on our own.

We like to think of our money helping affect the life of at least one other person, such as helping one extra woman deal with abuse, or go to job training, or one extra child have a good place to go to school. This feeling of impact gives us great satisfaction.

DONOR CIRCLES In the 1990s the Ms. Foundation for Women and the Global Fund for Women pioneered a model called Donor Circles. In these programs the organization creates significant pools of money with gifts of $5,000–$1 million each from major donors for specific projects or interest areas. The donor circle is often staffed by the sponsoring agency or foundation, which generally requires 20 to 35 percent of the income given to manage overhead and expansion for the circle. Aside from administrative tasks, these costs support a high level of donor engagement, offering donors learning opportunities through site visits or inservice trainings so that they can deepen their expertise in giving. Such long-term donor education results in expanded commitment to an area of funding or partnership with the sponsoring agency. Donor circles generally consist of ten to twenty-five donors or their representatives who meet three to five times a year to deepen partnerships and collective knowledge between themselves, staff, and advisors.

After two years of being a member of a donor circle affiliated with an abused women's center, one donor commented on her increased commitment: "I feel as though I am now a donor activist on this issue. In fact, not only will I give more to the battered women's shelter that sponsored this, but I will be a champion of this cause in getting friends and more community involved. I also have decided to make a legacy gift in my will to the organization. I have been that moved."

E-Philanthropy and e-volunteerism

E-philanthropy is the widely accepted umbrella term for nonprofit and philanthropic activity on-line, which includes the relatively new practices of e-giving, e-fundraising, and e-advocacy. This on-line space is quickly emerging as a community of interest poised to become a self-organizing community of practice. These on-line entities are new enterprises introducing new ways to give and volunteer, increase organizational effectiveness, and find information and supporters. At these sites visitors may make a financial contribution, volunteer time, sign a petition, or log an opinion.

Ideas that are possible only because of technology are providing new, innovative approaches to philanthropy and service. Sites like www.givenation.com and www.ebay.com make it possible to create a personal site for family and friends to give to their favorite charity. Click-and-give sites make it possible for anyone—including children—to "raise" money, and www.volunteermatch.org helps people of all ages to participate in volunteer activities on-line. Virtual volunteers serve on-line as they help organizations to develop databases, monitor bulletin boards, send out e mailings, and design or maintain Web sites, or they can help individual people through online tutoring, mentoring, and conversation. Issue-oriented and affinity sites research the nonprofit world to find high-performing organizations, then encourage individual donors who have voiced an interest with the particular issue to fund them.

For more information and a searchable database of sites, we recommend the Web page Knowledgeworks on e-Philanthropy, which is located on the Alliance for Community Technology Web site (www.communitytechnology.org) and is a partnership between that organization and the W.K. Kellogg Foundation. Their report, *e-Philanthropy v2001: From Entrepreneurial Adventure to an Online Community,* categorizes four major forms of on-line philanthropy:

- "Click-and-give" sites, where commercial sponsors promise to give cash to designated organizations when individuals visit the site. The Hunger Site, for example, operated by Greater Good, raised $3.5 million in 2000 to fight hunger worldwide. Each time a visitor at www.hungersite.org clicks a "donate today" button, one of Great Good's sponsors donates the equivalent of a cup of rice. A page of the sponsors then appears, with links to their shopping sites.

- Online shopping sites, where some portion of the profit on the purchased items is donated to charity. There are on-line malls where groups of stores agree to participate together.

- Portal sites, which aggregate organizations working on similar causes and vet them to the potential donor.

- Business-to-business services in on-line fundraising offered to nonprofits by consulting and technology companies.

Many nonprofits are also experimenting with ways to work on-line to deliver their mission-related services. These include advocacy actions such as virtual petitions and letter-writing campaigns on social movement issues, tools and coaching aimed at improving organizational effectiveness, volunteer matching and management, virtual volunteering through providing human and social services on-line, and e-education and programming for children and youth.

At the time of this writing, www.ePhilanthropyFoundation.org is the only infrastructure support organization of this emerging industry. Devoted to fostering secure, ethical, and private on-line philanthropy, it has developed a code of ethical philanthropic practices and is learning about and sharing good practice models.

The expanse and variety of options of on-line activity are expected to grow, along with greater depth in the sophistication and complexity of services and multiplication of links that enable many bases of information and people to be easily accessible.

Venture philanthropy

In the past decade, a new generation of business entrepreneurs has joined the effort to address social issues. These donors, referred to as venture philanthropists, apply the principles and practices of venture capitalism to the nonprofit sector, including long-term partnerships and strategic management assistance to leverage and augment financial investments. Although one researcher noted that the venture phi-

On-line philanthropy: Ideas for action

- Do your on-line shopping at Web sites that donate a percentage of your purchase to charity.
- Give money directly via secure transactions at the Web sites of organizations you want to support.
- Learn more about issues and organizations you may want to be involved with.
- Volunteer time, talent, and service.
- Participate in social advocacy and action.
- Learn about community-based fundraising events.

lanthropy field is "so diverse and unsettled it resembles the Wild West," several of the existing venture philanthropy models share a number of characteristics:

- Donors refer to themselves as investors.
- Investors initiate projects by convening people and resources and also respond to requests for funding.
- Investment is long term (three to six years) rather than year-to-year.
- Investors act as managing partners rather than checkbook partners.
- Investors require ongoing accountability rather than follow-up evaluation.
- Investors provide cash, expertise, and problem-solving, and closely monitor projects.
- Investors plan their exit or transition from the partnership from the beginning.

In practice, venture philanthropy models range widely, from multi-donor funds that adhere closely to the practices of venture capitalists to foundations of wealthy individuals that, while new, actually operate much like traditional grantmakers. A report by the Morino Institute suggests three broad categories of venture philanthropy:

• Venture-generated philanthropic funds, in which the resources being distributed are contributed from successful venture capital efforts, while disbursement of the funds is not necessarily made according to principles a venture capitalist would follow.

• Venture-influenced philanthropic funds, in which the philanthropy reflects at least some of the characteristics of venture capital.

• Venture-parallel philanthropic funds, in which there is a high level of engagement reflected in matching financial investment with strategic management assistance. These funds make fewer but larger investments and usually have larger staffs to provide management assistance and capacity building to recipients.

Aided by the rising stock market of the 1990s and high hopes for more partners, major foundations even started the Foundation Incubator in the heart of the Silicon Valley in Northern California, replicating the venture capital small business incubator models, to support and staff the creation of new foundations.

Venture philanthropists refer to the nonprofit partners in whom they invest as social entrepreneurs. Social entrepreneurs are typically described as nonprofit professionals who deliver and sustain services in an entrepreneurial way and who welcome the opportunity to work with business partners to achieve results.

Venture philanthropists attempt to counter the under-capitalization of infrastructure that leaves many nonprofits in a constant state of struggle. They point out that traditional foundations tie funds directly to the organization's programs, while leaving it to the nonprofit to find the additional funds necessary to support operational effectiveness. As a result, many nonprofits are unable to raise funds to improve their computer systems and data infrastructure or recruit and train qualified staff.

Some critics point out that concepts that work well in business don't always translate into societal change, where multiple factors, such as poverty, drug addiction, and high rates of transience can make measurement of single interventions, for example in health services, extremely difficult at best. As with most new arenas, there is a learning curve to negotiate before the best aspects of venture philanthropy can merge with and perhaps improve nonprofit approaches.

Social venture partners

Essential to the process of being a venture philanthropist are learning opportunities. One such group, Social Venture Partners, has served as a solid incubator for convening and experimentation in the Pacific Northwest, backyard of Microsoft, where its founders came from. Social Venture Partners (SVP) is a nonprofit, volunteer-driven organization dedicated to addressing social and environmental issues in the King County region of Washington. Each Social Venture Partner commits to a minimum annual contribution of $5,500 for at least two years.

Social Venture Partners are committed to providing whatever it takes to help bolster the success of each of the nonprofit groups they are involved with. Such involvement ranges from hands-on work, such as mentoring a child or setting up a Web site, to management support in the areas of finance, strategic planning, fund development, legal, marketing, and more. Although partners are not required to contribute time and expertise, more than two-thirds do.

Most of the work takes place in small groups of partners who research social and environmental issues, make investment decisions, and organize volunteer, capacity-building efforts to help investees. Since SVP was launched in 1997, they have granted more than $3.4 million and provided tens of thousands of hours of volunteer time and expertise to twenty-eight nonprofit organizations.

SVP also offers a range of information, workshops, and resources to further develop the personal philanthropy of its partners. Speakers share their expertise on topics such as creating personal giving plans, social entrepreneurship, and specific social issues such as children's programs, education, and the environment. By informing and educating its partnership, SVP hopes to catalyze the philanthropic potential of the Puget Sound region. It is also modeling itself globally through its Web site (svp_seattle.org) and trainings.

Nonprofit venture forums

Nonprofit venture forums represent a new model of showcasing nonprofit groups that you may want to investigate replicating in your community. The most prominent example is organized by a group called Craigslist Foundation.

Craigslist Foundation is a part of www.craigslist.org, an online community in fourteen U.S. cities as well as in Sydney and Melbourne, Australia. The foundation's stated mission is "to expand community-based philanthropy by actively engaging community members and small, young nonprofits in ways that build engaged relationships, educate donors, and support the work of the nonprofits." One of its programs is called Nonprofit Venture Forums. These events connect local nonprofits with philanthropists who want to learn more and become involved.

Their first nonprofit venture forum generated funding and resources for small, social change organizations and educated donors about a variety of new groups. In one year, the organization hosted six nonprofit venture fairs (five in the San Francisco Bay Area and one in Boston), giving thirty-six nonprofits the opportunity to present their solutions to community issues to more than 200 diverse members of the giving community. A wide range of donors with capacity to make donations of at least $250 were invited to each of these venture fairs. Each evening focuses on a different topic. For example, one night youth-led groups present their programs, another night cultural arts, a third focuses on international programs, and so on.

In preparation for the fairs, some thirty to one hundred applicant organizations apply to a steering committee to be showcased; the top ten groups are interviewed by the committee. Of these, six are chosen and helped to prepare for their presentations with technical assistance and group and media support. On their evening, each group has ten minutes to present their work followed by five minutes of questions from the prospective donor audience. The donors come prepared with a packet on each group, which includes a pledge form with which they can make donations that evening.

In all, the six fairs in one year produced more than $160,000 in cash grants, along with donations of pro bono services and the acquisition of board members and even office space. Another benefit was the consultation the sixty finalists received in presenting their case. Donors, too, benefit from this new way to learn about local issues and their possible solutions and to be introduced to social change organizations they might never have known about.

Progressive public foundations:
Practicing community-based philanthropy

Over the course of the 1900s, what was commonly thought of as philanthropic giving expanded from being the purview of a handful of wealthy industrialists and business owners seeking to balance their amassed wealth with public charity to incorporating a more broad-based involvement. The United Way, begun in the 1920s, was the first large organization to pool donors' funds and distribute them to community projects. The creation of traditional Community Foundations followed, building permanent philanthropic assets in particular geographic areas. As Community Foundations attracted unrestricted donations, they could distribute those funds to established health, human services, arts, and education institutions.

Beginning in the 1960s and 1970s, an even more democratic form of organized philanthropy emerged. Women, people of color, and others whose issues and organizations were not being supported by traditional foundations and the United Way forged new ground by creating community-based public foundations whose missions were to support grassroots organizations working specifically for positive societal change.

These public foundations differ from other funders in their distinctive practices of how giving is done and where it goes. Democratic governance structures ensure that decision-making bodies are representative of the communities served by the foundations' programs. Often, donors and activists make decisions together, allocating grants according to the combined wisdom of a diverse group of people. They support organizations whose work addresses the root causes of social, economic, and environmental problems. For example, while a traditional charity might fund a homeless shelter, a community-based foundation might fund community groups working on policy issues related to affordable housing, services for the mentally ill, and living wage standards. In this way, community-based philanthropy is working to address the underlying issues that lead to homelessness as a social problem.

In the late 1990s, a national, publicly supported foundation called Changemakers was founded to help promote community-based philanthropy efforts.

Providing guidance for the field of community-based philanthropy, Change-makers has developed the following set of values that it sees community-based philanthropic organizations incorporating in their work:

Accountable: Practicing honesty and transparency and answering to a wider community

Compassionate: Being motivated to uplift all beings

Inclusive: Valuing all people equally and treating people with respect regardless of their race, culture, religion, language, immigration history, age, class, sexual orientation, gender, or disabilities

Democratic: Involving a broad range of constituencies in decision-making processes

Strategic: Addressing root causes of social, economic, and environmental problems, often with innovative and creative approaches

Collaborative: Working in partnership with like-minded organizations and building bridges between donors and grantees

Because community-based philanthropy helps to build local movements for social change, these foundations are closely tied to the communities they serve and are often the first place new, small, or cutting-edge organizations turn for financial support. During the last decade, the number of community-based public foundations has grown, now including more than two hundred organizations encompassing broad social justice funds; women's funds; funds serving lesbian, gay, bisexual, and transgendered populations; and funds in communities of color.

These are community institutions in the broadest sense. Not only do they make grants, they often act as a nexus for networking and community organizing. They also offer opportunities for donors to engage in meaningful ways with people of different classes, races, religions, and cultures. Most major cities have at least one such organization that would welcome you as a donor or volunteer.

Community-based workplace funds and federations

More than 175 workplace funds and federations expand access to community-based giving through the workplace for donors who are interested in the democratization of philanthropy. Funds solicit for their member agencies or grantees, which include health agencies, community development organizations, neighborhood groups, environmental protection projects, organizations working on nonviolence, arts and cultural organizations, women's groups, and a multitude of identity groups, including African Americans, Hispanics, Native Americans, Asian Americans, and gay/lesbian/transgendered people.

This movement is growing rapidly. According to "Workplace Fundraising Data, 1996, 1998 & 1999 Campaign," by the National Committee on Responsive Philanthropy, employee contributions to the progressive community-based funds—which include Black United Funds, environmental funds, social action funds, and women's funds—increased by 23 percent between 1996 and 1999, while nationally the United Way's campaign totals, including employee contributions, major donor, and corporate gifts for the same period, increased by only 12 percent.

If your workplace doesn't have giving options through payroll deduction, we urge you to contact your local community-based workplace fund or federation or United Way about initiating a campaign. Inquire whether the fund you give to includes groups that match your values and perspectives on social reform. If not, ask for more choice in the programs being offered. The National Alliance for Choice in Giving (see Resources) can give you more information about your local or statewide environmental funds, Black United Funds, women's funds, the Native American Rights Fund, United Latino Fund, and social action funds.

Public foundations and community-based workplace funds are among the most effective methods for donors to assure that their money is being distributed democratically. Funds are pooled and redistributed based on a thoughtful and ethical process through committees that include representatives of the communities being served.

Chapter 11

Encouraging children
to give

■   ■   ■

Only a few years ago there were few resources to help parents and children think about giving and service. Happily, more and more resources and tools are being developed. Imagine the impact that expanding kids' consciousness and excitement about the nonprofit sector will have. This chapter discusses some of those resources and gives some inspiring examples of children and youth reaching out to make their communities better places.

The Council of Michigan Foundations and the Milwaukee Women's Fund have done some terrific work in developing programs for kids relating to giving and service. The Web site www.learningtogive.org contains the Council of Michigan Foundations' extensive development of a giving and service curriculum that is now being used in many schools nationwide. The site also has other excellent ideas and resources. At www.dollardiva.com, a Web site of the institution Independent Means, young women have the chance to think about money, community service, and giving.

We suggest that you start early to tell your children stories about giving and service that will inspire the values you want them to have. You may also want to begin a home library of books that inform and inspire you or your kids about giving (see Appendix F, Resources). In particular, we feel that children need to understand that giving and volunteering create community and help develop what are perhaps the most powerful skills one needs in life: team building, listening, and empathy. Not only is empathy an antidote for narcissism, it's the way we will create a more compassionate and caring world.

The following two stories tell how young people are being taught by family members to be givers.

Sarah Silber: Growing up giving

From the time I was born, I received small gifts of money on my birthday and at Hanukkah. When I was nine, my parents opened a special "gift" account for me and began teaching me the meaning of the account's interest and balance figures. When I was 16, my grandmother encouraged me to begin contributing some of my savings (then $3,200) and my time to projects that interested me. My grandmother made a deal with me: for every hour I volunteered and for every dollar I gave of my own money, my grandmother would contribute a dollar to my "Giving Fund" for future use.

I began keeping newspaper and magazine articles, brochures, and flyers about issues and groups that interested me. After a while I noticed that most of the information I had collected was about dolphins and abused children. I realized that one way I could help in these areas was to give money to the projects that excited me. To help me understand how groups would use my donations, I made a list of groups I had read about and looked them up at the library. I found that three of the organizations on my list that work to rehabilitate injured dolphins were mentioned in a book on national environmental nonprofits. I also learned about the Environmental Support Center in Washington, D.C., and wrote to them for more information. With all this information, I began making some donations.

Now 23, I get a sense of the groups I support or might begin supporting through reading their mailings or visiting the projects themselves. My list has gone beyond dolphins and abused children, and I keep files alphabetically by organization, with a contact sheet for each to remind me of me past ideas and actions with the groups. I sometimes make donations to organizations in honor of friends or other family members. Since I turned 18, I have been giving away $300 a year.

I have developed my own funding cycle, writing checks twice a year: around the time of my birthday and the year-end holidays. Since I collect and file information all year, I spend only about twenty minutes at the end of each year creating my plan. The plan helps me stay focused and keep my priorities clear, and it makes it easier to turn down requests for donations outside of my giving categories and funding cycles.

Wendy Stewart: Holiday giving

One of my giving strategies is to teach my nieces and nephews about philanthropy. Starting when they are around age nine, I call them at Christmas and explain that I'm giving them a certain number of dollars to give away this year. (Their parents and I decide the amount together. I don't want to give an amount that would make their parents uncomfortable, and this also gives their parents a way to participate.) I then begin to talk with each child about their interests and concerns about the world. With young kids, I think it's important not to get too heavy about this; I don't want them to give out of guilt or to feel they must begin carrying the weight of the world. But I want to find something that will be meaningful to them.

This has been a great project for a number of reasons. First, I get to hear what my nieces and nephews are interested in and concerned about (or not concerned about); I get to know them better. Second, it's our project, something they do with Aunt Wendy. Third, when they're older, we can begin to talk about philanthropy. For example, we'll talk about whether they want to give the money in one gift or split it into several gifts. This could spark a conversation about making small donations compared with bigger impacts. And in the course of deciding where to give the money, we can begin discussing what makes for strategic giving.

Teenage initiatives

Teenagers can be particularly avid activists and their philanthropic initiatives can be found everywhere. The following are some inspired examples based on teens following their values and passions. We hope they will spark ideas for you or a teenager in your life.

Ten ways families can encourage kids' spirit of generosity

■   ■   ■   ■   ■   ■   ■   ■   ■   ■   ■   ■   ■   ■

1. Model abundance or sufficiency, not fear, secrecy, and inadequacy.
2. Talk about giving, volunteering, and service and demonstrate each.
3. Be a mentor with your children about money and giving or find one early on.
4. Set giving, volunteering, and work ethic standards early on.
5. Teach responsible budgeting, planning, and checkbook and credit card management.
6. Set up a giving account for contributions and seed it with money, and give ongoing age-appropriate guidance.
7. Provide motivation for anonymous gifts and generosity.
8. Balance needs and wants with global understanding and consideration. Know where your family is on the economic spectrum, and help your kids to understand what that means.
9. Create a family giving plan and include your kids' values and priority issues and concerns for their (and your) communities.
10. Increase your community service hours. The national average for Americans is more than 150 hours per year. More volunteering and less TV or computer time might open the hearts and minds of your whole family.

A center for newcomers

Graciella Villa Franca had grown up noticing that her Latina relatives were always extending food and helpful community information to new neighbors or visitors to their small town near Tucson, Arizona. But she realized early on that something more had to be done. New immigrants needed more care than her relatives and the local government agencies were providing. She came up with the idea of a center for new immigrants and refugees and at age 13 gathered her friends together and met with the local town council.

Building relationships with mentors and other adults, she began fundraising each Saturday for her vision. She and her friends involved their families, friends, and local officials to help. Graciella even found an architect who produced a drawing for a building and center that included her dream, apartments for temporary housing for seven families. Over the next five years, Graciella and her cousin were part of more than thirty-five community fundraising events. Today, thanks to the persistence and vision of one teenager and a lot of help and effort by others, the center has been built. Twenty-four teens from the area play a key role in providing welcoming and referral services.

The poetry slam

The poetry slam was Lin Chao's idea. She had seen a program on her local public TV station about hip hop and decided it was time for a space in her community where a group of young people could read or recite and move to their poetry and hip hop. At a local library, she found an upstairs room that was rarely used and got permission for a Friday night poetry slam. First twenty, and then more than fifty kids came. Local bookstores helped Lin and her friends publicize the weekly event and in exchange sold books and hip hop CDs at the slams. A local stereo and audio store donated a microphone for the kids to use in exchange for publicity at the event. From that spark, and with no funds needed, one town's teens have a sage and fun place to express themselves.

Youth as grantmakers

Some philanthropic institutions are also bringing young people into philanthropy to help with youth-related funding. Local community foundations have pioneered Youth Advisory Committees (YACs) as a new model of youth-directed philanthropy. A YAC assesses local youth needs in order to recommend grants from a designated youth fund. Foundations tend to recruit young people to such committees from varied racial, socioeconomic, and academic backgrounds—including those who aren't already school leaders—in hopes of making their groups representative of the community. The young people research potential recipients of funding and make giving recommendations. Sometimes the youth advisors are also involved in raising money for the fund.

YACs provide community foundations with a peer perspective on youth programs and youth-related needs in the community and allow young people a direct say in deciding where charitable money should go. YACs also give foundations an opportunity to teach teenagers about philanthropy, with the hope that they will be more likely to be involved in giving as they get older.

In Rochester, New York, for example, six teenagers and two adult advisors work within the Rochester Area Community Foundation to hand out $10,000 a year in grants of up to $750 each to fund programs run by youth peers. "In the history of charitable organizations, young people who came to us were often viewed as problems needing to be addressed, as kids-at-risk," says Jennifer Leonard, who heads the foundation. "In the last ten years, there's been a large mind-shift," she says. "That mind-shift looks at young people as potential sources of great strength for themselves, their families, and communities."

In another example, the Community Foundation of Silicon Valley (California) recruits high school students from the communities of East Palo Alto and East San Jose, less prosperous communities bordering some of the country's most affluent neighborhoods, to their Youth In Philanthropy committee. In 2001 the committee gave away about $20,000—nearly 15 percent of which they raised themselves—to youth-initiated projects.

"The whole concept of philanthropy is pretty new to most of them," says adviser Julie Dean. "They're tough grant-makers. By the time they get to the end, they're asking really good questions about groups' motivations, and grilling them on their budgets. They learn a lot of critical thinking skills."

Many high school students are now raising money and giving it away through a similar model within their schools. If you are a young person you may want to think about forming or looking into possibilities of joining this kind of group; if you are an adult you may want to help fund a YAC. For more information about Youth Advisory Councils, see the Web site www.ysa.org.

A new curriculum on the Internet from ruMAD in Melbourne, Australia encourages high school students to participate in their program, Making a Difference. The curriculum instructs students and teachers in developing action projects and establishing school-based youth foundations (see www.rumad.org.au).

Young people ask about giving

Like adults, young people can have conflicts of interest, limited time, and questions about how best to use their resources. Here are some questions young people have asked us about how to make choices that reflect the world they care about, along with some suggested answers.

Q: I want to volunteer my time for issues that interest me but I'm not really sure I can take the time away from homework and everything else I'm doing at school. I'd also like to earn some money.

A: Having a balanced life is important. Getting involved with things you care about is exciting and will inspire the rest of your life. You may need to make choices about your extracurricular priorities in order to do everything. Also, for most people, the busier you are the more efficient you are with your time and getting things done. Volunteer work with an organization or project gives you some experience, knowledge about the work, and contacts that could lead to some paid hours.

Q: When I volunteer, I always seem to get the busywork. How can I get other experiences?

A: A lot of volunteering is doing basic tasks, but there can also be variety. Watch others and the volunteer jobs they have, then ask your supervisor for more and varied experiences. You can also call a local volunteer center or talk with a teacher at school about wanting other experience. The key is to know and be able to articulate your skills and offerings (see Exercise 2.4 in Chapter Two).

Q: My parents tell me to save my money for college, but I want to help out some of my friends or donate to help change the world. What can I do?

A: Keep a record of how much you earn or get for allowance and how much you spend. Then consider how you might shift things around so that you can allocate your time or dollars to fulfill both your own dreams and those your parents may have for you. Ask your parents if they feel comfortable with you donating a portion of your allowance or using it for gifts. And think about what seems like a good giving level: how about 5 percent for friends and gifting, 5 percent for nonprofit organizations that are trying to change the world? Parents and grandparents have the right to share their opinions and wisdom, but money you earn for allowance is up to you to allocate to the things that matter to you.

Q: I know I am spending money on CDs and supplies or extra clothes for school that I really don't need. How can I stop overspending or wasting?

A: Consider when you get your allowance or get pay for work you do dividing the money right away and putting it into envelopes. The envelopes might be labeled "money to save," "money to give," "money to spend," and "money to invest or lend." Even the spending money could be divided into "money to spend on essentials" and "money to spend on extra stuff." It's good to realize that, like others, you sometimes waste. The key is to know you can change and to try to do so. Also try giving to others or donating some of the extra stuff you have accumulated. There are many organizations that collect clothing, toys, and the like and redistribute them to needy children. You can also make cash donations to these groups. Or hold a garage sale with some of your friends and donate the money you earn that day to a cause you care about.

Q: I want to help women and children who are refugees or immigrants. How can I do that?

A: There are many Web sites that can help you find international resources. Start by thinking about what difference you want to make internationally. Do you want to help people who need basic food, shelter, or medical support? Or do you want to learn more about changing some of the policies that cause people to migrate from their countries or become refugees? Here are a few resources you can start with:

www.globalfundforwomen.org

www.iearn.org

www.internationaldonors.org

www.justgive.org

Chapter 12

For donors who have $25,000 or more to give

■ ■ ■

People with high net worth have even greater opportunities to share their abundance with the nonprofit sector, giving to and even spearheading programs and organizations that reflect their deepest wishes for the world. As with any giving described in this book, giving large amounts of money each year will be both more effective and more satisfying if it is done thoughtfully based on your interests and values.

When making decisions about how much you can and want to give, consulting with financial advisors and funding peers can be invaluable for developing systematic ways of thinking about your giving and for getting emotional and practical support.

This chapter presents a number of resources that may be helpful in thinking about how much to give and where, and in learning more about issues and the groups that address them.

Working with an advisor

Your giving is likely be more successful if you work with a financial professional to know and understand your spending, your cash flow, and the creative and wise timing and uses of your assets. An industry of wealth advisors, investment advisors, financial and estate planners, accountants, lawyers, and philanthropic advisors is available to give advice about establishing giving programs (see Resources). Working with good advisors will help you to assess your assets, both material and leadership, so that you are aware of your capacities and limitations.

Choose an advisor who has at least some shared values, is a good communicator, and will honor and add value to your work as a donor or philanthropist. Giving takes time and care; clear, realistic goals; and patience.

These are some questions an advisor might ask in an initial meeting; preparing your answers ahead of time will enable you to get the most out of the consultation.

- What do you want your legacy to be? What would you like your giving to say about who you are and what you believe?
- Have you considered ways to spark giving during your lifetime with your children or other family members?
- How much time do you want to devote to philanthropy? Do you know the services that we provide and what they cost?
- How much do you want to leave to the next generation and how do you want it distributed?
- What role would you like me to play in supporting your philanthropy?
- What referrals can I provide that would be useful?
- In looking at the balance of your taxable income and philanthropic deductions, do you know how much of your income and assets can you afford to give away?

Here are some initial questions that you may want to ask an advisor:

- What amount of money can I afford to give annually and at the time of my death that would best benefit my tax obligation and estate plan?

- At what point in the year can you give me estimates and a year-end figure for the maximum dollar amount I will be able to give to nonprofits and receive tax deductions?

- What are the pros and cons of giving through different vehicles?

- Can you help me establish charitable legacy or estate gifts that will benefit my community, my family, and my friends?

- Should I give appreciated stock instead of writing a check?

In additional to professional advice about financial and philanthropic management, on a practical day-to-day level you may want to hire an assistant to help you organize and get to know your paperwork, or ask part of your existing or family's financial team to help you.

Table 12.1, created by the Minnesota Council on Foundations, provides a summary comparison of financial characteristics of some of the major types of charitable giving options covered in Chapter Ten. If your work with an advisor involves considering structured vehicles, we offer this chart as a useful starting point for choosing options.

Thinking about giving from net worth

One question that donors with high net worth often consider is whether to give from principal. In the past, donors were invariably advised to "conserve principal." This is no longer the only wise choice. Investment manager, donor, and author of *Wise Giving*, Claude Rosenberg has created a Web site for donors and investment advisors (www.newtithing.org) that presents a method for calculating what he calls "affordable charitable giving levels." Rosenberg makes a compelling case, backed up by state-by-state statistics, that most of those holding the top 2 percent of American assets can afford to more than double their giving without significantly impairing their wealth. The One Percent Club in Minnesota is proving his point.

TABLE 12.1 Giving Options Compared.

	Charitable Giving Option					
	Make a Direct Gift to a Charity	Create a Family or Private Foundation	Give to or Through a Community or Public Foundation (Donor-Advised Funds)	Develop a Corporate Giving Program, Foundation, or Fund	Create a Supporting Organization	Join or Form a Giving or Donor Circle
1. Donor can control investment of assets	No	Yes	No	Yes	Limited	Limited[1]
2. Donor can control giving priorities	Yes[2]	Yes	Limited[3]	Yes	Limited	Limited[1]
3. Likelihood of being perpetual	Low[4]	High	High	NA	High	Low
4. By virtue of gift, donor may control who serves on governing board	No[5]	Yes	No[5]	Yes	Limited	Yes, usually
5. Requires donor time and effort, plus expense of staff and management	No	Yes	No[7]	Yes	Yes	Yes[6]
6. Minimum payout required and realized capital gains	No	Yes	No, though 5% minimally recommended of assets per year	Yes, if a foundation	No	Yes
7. Must pay 1–2 percent tax on investment income and realized capital gains	No	Yes	No	Yes, if a foundation[10]	No	No
8. Tax deduction limited for gifts of cash (percent of adjusted gross income that may be deducted)	50%[8]	30%[8]	50%[8]	10% of pre-tax profits[8]	50%[8]	50%[8]

Charitable Giving Option

	Make a Direct Gift to a Charity	Create a Family or Private Foundation	Give to or Through a Community or Public Foundation (Donor-Advised Funds)	Develop a Corporate Giving Program, Foundation, or Fund	Create a Supporting Organization	Join or Form a Giving or Donor Circle
9. Tax deduction limitation for gifts of stock or real property (percent of adjusted gross income that may be deducted)	30%	20%[8,9]	30%[8]	10% of pre-tax profits[8]	30%[8]	30%[8]
10. Valuation of gifts of property other than publicly traded stock	Fair market value	Cost basis	Fair market value	Cost-basis, if a foundation	Fair market value	NA [11]
11. Separate tax return required and open to public inspection	No	Yes	No	Yes, if foundation	Yes	No

Adapted from Minnesota Toolkit for Giving www.minnesotagiving.org.(Contact an advisor for updated tax information or verification.)

1. Legal structures of giving circles vary, resulting in different levels of donor control. Pooling resources with others also limits direct personal control.

2. Charity and donor can agree on how contribution is spent.

3. A restricted gift can be confined to the stated purpose, but the donor relinquishes control of the investment and its disposition. A donor-advised fund permits the donor to make recommendations subject to the control of the community foundation.

4. Except when you create an endowment.

5. Any citizen may be elected or appointed to the board of any public charity. The donor gift does not guarantee such an outcome except in the case of supporting organizations.

6. Giving circles vary in requirements for involvement and in management structure and cost.

7. Community foundations often assess a management or administrative fee.

8. Excess in any year's donation can be carried forward for five years.

9. Except for gifts of publicly traded stock, the deductible value of lifetime gifts of closely held stock or real property is limited to tax basis, which is generally cost.

10. Corporate foundations must pay the same excise tax as any private foundation.

11. Giving circles typically accept donations of cash and stock only.

The One Percent Club is a voluntary association of Minnesotans with high net worth who have committed to give annually 1 percent or more of their net worth or 5 percent of their income, whichever is greater, to the worthy cause(s) of their choice. The underlying idea for the club is that giving should be based on a percentage of net worth; members state that having a 1 percent benchmark has brought discipline to their giving. Founded in 1997, the group's goal was to have 2,000 members by the end of 2002.

Tom Lowe founded the group. The next year, he studied 1997 IRS documents to see how much money wealthy Minnesotans had given away that year. From those figures, Lowe estimated that if the 32,000 households with an annual income of $200,000 or more were to give 1 percent of their net worth, they would be donating as much as $250 million more each year than they had in 1997. After its first year, the One Percent Club found that its members had given $7 million more to charities than the previous year.

Rosenberg urges donors to move their money themselves and reap enormous enjoyment or fall prey to Uncles Sam's distributions by government taxes. There may also be a tax advantage to giving appreciated assets. Exercise 12.1 uses the same concept as Exercise 5.2, "How Much Should You Give?" in Chapter Five, but from the perspective of giving from net worth. We urge you to include equity in calculating your philanthropic budget.

Networking with other major donors

When we exchange ideas, information, and experiences, we also help inspire and create solutions for each other and the world. This collective experience transforms us. Money becomes a tool that can change your life and help others change theirs.

—Tracy Hewat

Giving has been for many people a private matter. It can be a spiritual, creative, and centering process, but it can also be a chaotic, unbalancing, and isolated one. Increasingly, donors who want to learn from others are joining networks, attending conferences, and enrolling in courses on giving to connect with other donors

Giving from Assets

10 minutes

In thinking about what percentage of your net worth you want to give, you might start by looking at the table below. Find an approximation of your net worth; then look across the row until you see the amount you would like to give away. Look at the top of the table to see what percentage that is. Do the amount and the percentage feel right to you? If not, where is the disparity? If you have given in the past, what percentage of your net worth does your past giving represent? How does it compare with the amount or percentage in the table?

If your net worth is	and you want to give					
	1%	3%	5%	10%	15%	20%
$250,000	2,500	7,500	12,500	25000	37500	50,000
$500,000	5,000	15,000	25,000	50,000	75,000	100,000
$750,000	7,500	22,500	37,500	75,000	112,500	150,000
$1,000,000	10,000	30,000	50,000	100,000	150,000	200,000
$2,000,000	20,000	60,000	100,000	200,000	300,000	400,000
$4,000,000	40,000	120,000	200,000	400,000	600,000	800,000
$5,000,000	50,000	150,000	250,000	500,000	750,000	1,000,000
$10,000,000	100,000	300,000	500,000	1,000,000	1,500,000	2,000,000
$20,000,000	200,000	600,000	1,000,000	2,000,000	3,000,000	4,000,000

This year I/we want to give $_____, which represents _____ percent of my/our net worth.

Next year I/we want to give $_____, which represents _____ percent of my/our net worth.

and learn more about the art and craft of philanthropy. As many donors are anonymous, being identified in a meeting as a donor makes some people feel vulnerable. "Will everyone ask me for money or assume I have or give more than I do?" is the usual fear that keeps many donors from going to community presentations that will inform their giving. If you will need to identify yourself at such a meeting, you can protect your funding position by saying something like, "I'm interested in learning more about this issue."

There are many gatherings and opportunities available to donors across a spectrum of philanthropic budgets; they fall into the following types:

- Donors meeting together in groups, usually with others at their economic or giving level

- Foundation staff and donors meeting to share experiences and ideas or to make site visits together to community groups

- Donor and activist or community groups meeting to examine or discuss how some specific problem might be addressed

- Donors and foundation staff or board members sharing learning or information on e-mail list serves or Web sites

- Activists meeting at conferences regarding a specific issue and considering whether they might work better collaboratively, or how they can describe their work to donors and funders more successfully

- Donors, activists, and foundation staff meeting together to discuss common problems and solutions

There are also more informal networks of donors from every population, issue, or affinity group you can imagine: younger donors; donors of color; women donors; environmental funders; gay, lesbian and bisexual donors; funders who give internationally; donors to the arts; and funders of disability issues. While most of these networks are for educational value primarily, some engage periodically in collaborative giving initiatives or donor or giving circles. There are enormous advantages to belonging to or attending some of these affinity groups or donor networks, including the following:

- Meeting a peer group with some shared values

- Engaging with others from a broader geographic area, which can be national or even international

- Good speakers, articles, and resources to learn from

- Idea exchange and networking

- Collaborative promoting or funding of the area, issue, or philanthropy in general

Donors or foundation staff with shared politics or interests also join funder networks to consider strategies, learn the basics together, or collaborate. Examples of some organizations through which you can access these forums are the Black Philanthropy Conference, the Environmental Grantmakers Association, the Jewish Funders Network, the Council on Foundations, and the Association for Small Foundations (see Appendix F, Resources). The bimonthly *Chronicle on Philanthropy* is also a good place to find listings of these forums.

The industry of donor education has expanded tremendously since the 1990s. Community or public foundations, local United Ways, and philanthropic support and consulting organizations around the country, such as Resourceful Women, The Philanthropic Initiative, More than Money, Changemakers, and Resource Generation hold informative programs for funders (again, see Resources). Banks and trust companies, wealth advisors, philanthropic advisors, and investment and estate advisors also hold occasional programs for clients and prospective clients. The Rockefeller Foundation, Hewlett Foundation, and Stanford University's M.B.A. program now offer courses for philanthropists.

One example of a donor network is Marin Independent Donors (MID) in Marin County, California. MID is an informal group of donors giving at least $10,000 a year. The group asks for dues of $100 to $1,000, depending on how much a donor gives to their community annually, to help defray mailing costs and pay speakers. These annual assessments are not tax deductible as contributions, but most members deduct them as expenses related to charitable giving (for example, through a foundation or as a related expense). A volunteer steering committee plans the quarterly programs, which include the following types of topics:

- How to involve your children in your giving

- What nonprofits really want from donors

- Matching your philanthropy to community needs

- Collaborating in your grantmaking

- Anonymity versus disclosure: pros and cons

- Historical role models in philanthropy, such as Madame C. J. Walker and Andrew Carnegie

Working closely with organizations you may fund: Budgets, visits, letters

Philanthropist Peter Kent told the magazine *More than Money* that he devised a few questions to help guide him in making his first big gift:

> When I made my first $100,000 gift to a nonprofit organization, it was a big stretch for me. I wanted to help the organization build its capacity to operate at a vastly different level than it had been. I knew I needed to think carefully about the amount I wanted to give and why.
>
> These six questions helped guide me to risk such a major gift:
>
> - Do I judge this area of work as critical?
> - Is it timely for the work of this organization to grow?
> - Will I be excited to build a relationship with this group for the next five or more years?
> - Do I trust and respect the leadership, including the staff and board?
> - Do I judge the organization's finances as solid?
> - Has the group done thorough strategic planning?

If you were posing these questions about making a large gift, you would need to learn more about the organization in question in some depth. Two steps you should consider taking are examining the organization's budget and making a site visit to see them in action and to ask some questions about how they operate.

Reviewing an organization's budget

If you're thinking of making a substantial gift to an organization you will want to have some detailed knowledge about the group's financial situation. One way to do this is to review their budget and balance sheet. Organizations are required to conduct financial audits if they have budgets of more than $250,000, and the audits are available to the public upon request. Those with budgets between $100,000 and $249,000 must be reviewed by accountants; you could request a copy of that review.

Because there is no standard way to prepare a budget, budgets vary in format from organization to organization. A budget for a start-up effort or for a very small grassroots organization may not be as detailed or extensive as that for a large, well-established organization.

Here are some things to look for in reviewing an organization's budget, adapted from *Robin Hood was Right,* by Chuck Collins and Pam Rogers:

- A variety of income sources or a plan to diversify funding to include individuals, foundations, and grassroots strategies such as bowl-a-thons and parties.

- Evidence of local community support in the form of member contributions or grassroots fundraising income.

- The budget as a reference point. Make sure it reflects what the group is and what it does. For example, has a statewide organization budgeted for statewide work by including travel expenses? If a group works in a low-income community, does its budget show that it is truly accessible to the community—through adequate childcare and transportation expenses, for example?

- The fact that some fundraising strategies not only cost money but also have programmatic benefit. This is particularly true of direct mail and special events, which raise visibility and educate the public. Remember that you have to spend money to raise money.

- The income side to see if there is a great deal of government or corporate funding. Does this funding place a constraint on the type of organizing the group performs?

- If there are accountability structures in place. Are there mechanisms in the organization for fiscal oversight? Who sets the direction for the organization, and what input do they have into financial decisions? Are the people who write checks the same as those who receive the checks?

- If the salaries line item is reasonable in terms of paying staff living wages with benefits. Look for salary differentials that indicate inequality among different staff positions. If a budget is all salaries, it can be a warning that the work is entirely staff-driven and that community involvement is lacking.

- Deficits. Look for big changes in income and expenses from one year to the next. Both these indicators can show instability.

Making a site visit

Another way to learn more deeply about how an organization functions is to see some of its work in action. If you have made or are planning a major gift, request a site visit. To make the best use of your time and that of the organization, use Worksheet 12.1 to come prepared to focus on what you want to learn.

Managing written communication

A lot of communication and relationship building between donors and groups goes on through letters or e-mail. Not only a direct way of communicating (no phone tag!), letters and e-mail also ensure that your wishes are clear and easily referred to. Appendix C contains a number of sample letters you may wish to use in various circumstances.

Preparing for Site Visits

Step 1. Preparation

- Define the goal of your site visit, such as to learn about the organization and its work, or to determine the appropriateness of a future or further gift.

- Read the proposal or background information.

- Think about your expectations, questions, and concerns in advance.

Step 2. Consider the questions you want to ask from among the following subject areas and possibilities:

Program and Leadership

- What is the organization's mission or primary purpose?

- What are you trying to accomplish?

- What are the organization's primary programs or activities and their immediate and long-range purposes?

- What is the organization's primary strategy to achieve those goals?

- What is the most exciting thing the group is doing now?

- How does your community perceive the organization's work?

History

- How long has the organization been doing what it does? Why was it formed? Has its mission or purpose changed during the past three to five years?

- What is the organization's vision for its work over the next year? Three years? Do you have a written and approved strategic plan? If so, may I have a copy? How and why do you see the work changing? What impact do you think your project has had on the issue the organization is addressing?

- Who does your organization serve? Who are your constituencies?

- Who is your leadership body? What kind of people and talent have been involved? How do you support your staff and board to develop their skills and awareness?

Organizational Functioning

- How many people work with and for the organization, in what capacities? Do board members, senior staff, and volunteers reflect your clients and other constituents?

- Who decides what? Are constituents involved in staff, board and volunteer leadership?

- How does your organization define success? How do you decide when to alter strategy or direction?

- Is there anything else you'd like me to know?

Fundraising

- What is your budget?

- How much is earned, how much is contributed?

- What are the organization's sources of earned and contributed income?

- What are your fundraising goals? Do you have a fundraising plan? Who is involved in fundraising?

- Does the organization have a cash reserve? How big is it as a proportion of the budget?

- Does the organization have an endowment? How large is it? What is its purpose?

- If I am unable to fund this project, or can only fund a percentage of your request, how will this affect its going forward?

- What is the most useful gift a donor or foundation could give you now?

_____

_____

_____

_____

_____

_____

_____

_____

_____

Afterword

Each of us must accept the challenge of leadership—leadership from within that unites the inner life of spirit with the outer life of service. When we do, we will discover what the great spiritual traditions have taught: simply, as we enhance our inner capacity for wholeness and freedom, we strengthen our outer capacity to love and serve. This is our common work. This is the call to the heart of philanthropy.

—Rob Lehman

After studying and participating in the world of philanthropy for many years, we have found that the most successful giving initiatives advance at least some (if not all) of the following values. We feel these could counterbalance some of our collective over-indulgences and self-interest of the past few decades:

- Truly democratized, community-based, philanthropy that engages the participation and concern of broad community interests

- A national budget that is sustainable and reflects family, community, national, and global needs

- A society that is educationally, economically, and financially literate

- Reasonable consumerism and minimal personal and national debt

- Reduced concentration of wealth and of tax benefits for the wealthy and for corporate America

- Increased involvement with other countries and cultures to address poverty and global strife

- A keener awareness of the global effects of our actions on the environment of each neighborhood and country

- A commitment at home and abroad to conflict mediation and peaceful, non-violent solutions

- A society that honors the sacredness of reflection and deep, soulful listening in balance with action

In their report from a recent exploratory conference on what is being called "Transformational Philanthropy," Duane Elgin and Elizabeth Share asked that donors and foundations consider the following questions:

- Does your grantmaking recognize that we have entered an historical time of change with a window of opportunity for innovation?

- Does your grantmaking take a whole-systems perspective? In other words, do you look at the changing dynamics of the global context as a framework for making strategic decisions?

- Does your grantmaking seek to build strength by actively embracing diversity and consciously seeking to build coalitions among diverse constituencies?

- Does your grantmaking imply a bigger story about human life and human purpose?

- Does your grantmaking foster self-organization at the grassroots scale?

- Does your grantmaking recognize and appreciate multiple ways of knowing?

As you make your donations of time and money, we urge you to continue to act on the following precepts:

- Think big, and take small, regular actions

- Act locally, nationally and internationally

- Fund collaborations and statewide and global initiatives

- Understand overarching policies and frameworks

- Learn with others to consider the systemic, root cause of problems and how they are connected, then integrate these findings into your philanthropy

- Mentor and nurture the next generation of givers and nonprofit workers

- Communicate with others about concerns, goals, and intentions

- Support leaders who are committed to transformative and collaborative efforts

- Cultivate change for broader civic engagement and democratic functionality through shifts in policy, research, the media, and the arts

- Be a force for fundraising and change for the issues and projects most central to your heart

- Give of yourself and your resources, knowing the certain guaranteed gifts of sufficiency and service

- Use the infrastructure of philanthropy—all the groups and networks in the Resource Section at the end of this book—as your own web of learning and support

- And finally, take the long-haul approach, knowing that the small acts you do today contribute to the cumulative impact of a life spent in sharing and caring

Take time to reflect and know what you hold most sacred and what you're called to co-create. It has taken the United States more than 200 years to develop the problems that it has. People of good will working together have always challenged oppressive institutions, and change has come slowly. Sometimes change has come and gone, and come again. To think that our efforts as philanthropists are going to have any visible effect is to fail to understand the nature of the long haul, and is to demand an immediate gratification that is one of the hallmarks of class privilege, but not of social justice.

Some final questions to reflect on

1. What have you learned from your own philanthropy to date?

2. What is your dream for humanity and how do you plan to participate in its manifestation?

3. What is something you hope to change in this new century and millennium?

As Reinhold Neibuhr reminds us,

■   ■   ■   ■   ■   ■   ■   ■   ■   ■   ■   ■   ■   ■   ■

Nothing worth doing can be accomplished in our lifetime; therefore we must be saved by hope. Nothing which is true or beautiful or good makes complete sense in any immediate context of history; therefore we must be saved by faith. Nothing we do, however virtuous, can be accomplished alone; therefore we must be saved by love. No virtuous act is quite as virtuous from the standpoint of friend or foe as it is from our standpoint. Therefore, we must be saved by the final favor of love, which is forgiveness.

4. Are you moved to consider more inspired giving? What will you do specifically?

5. What commitment will you make this year to bring more family, friends and colleagues to become "inspired philanthropists?"

Inspired philanthropy giving model

▪ ▪ ▪

The Inspired Philanthropy Giving Model places all philanthropic activity within the context of the cultural and social forces that influence us. Within that changing reality, our giving is based, first, on a combination of being rooted in our own values and passion and informed by community need to determine what we want to change, create, or affect.

We move then to assess potential nonprofit partners in alignment with our personal philanthropic mission, taking into account their mission and values and the quality of their leadership and previous efforts. These steps help us create our own giving plan, using it to support those causes and organizations we have come to care most about, as well as to use our leadership and influence on their behalf and to create partnerships with others working toward similar goals.

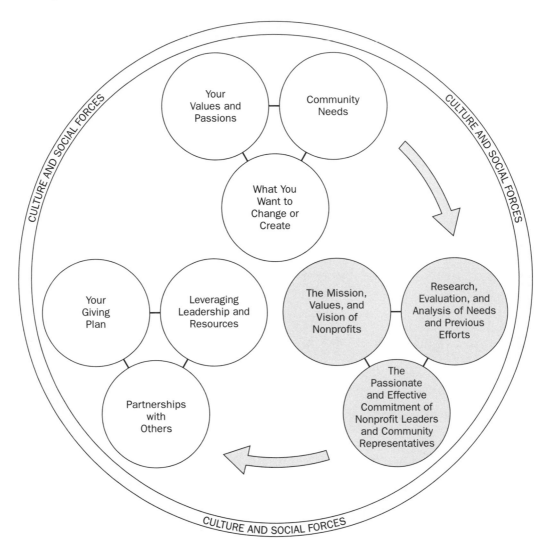

Figure A.1 Inspired Philanthropy Giving Model.

Creative ideas for giving

■ ■ ■

Giving away money is a serious business; it should also be fun. In the course of our work all over the country, we have encountered donors who have done many creative and interesting things with their gifts. One started a retreat and writing center. Another established a volunteer corps of professionals to work with small-budget nonprofits. Others established awards and memorial chairs in honor of their parents, created newsletters to keep a group of friends in touch, and started or seeded numerous nonprofits.

Here are some examples of creative givers and creative giving. We hope they stimulate your own creative thinking.

Making connections

Michal Feder an entrepreneurial donor and community catalyst. Some of her major gifts have been in the form of great ideas that have moved and sparked others' actions and mentorship, and she has nurtured them with expertise and guidance at critical junctures.

"I want to make the world a better place," says Michal (pronounced "Michael"), now a 76-year-old retired consultant. "But I'm an entrepreneur, a starter, not a holder or maintainer of projects. Knowing that about myself has given me great freedom and clarity to make better decisions."

Michal likes tangible results, lots of people physically involved and finally, a sense of completion. Her own assessment of the goals of some of her public service efforts is, "I look for projects where everyone benefits. I look for ideas whose time has come. I use my powers of persuasion and my abilities to make myself useful. And I hang in, within a reasonable time frame, to get the project done. That's my version of commitment! It's not about how much money or time I give, it's about using what I have in a timely, strategic, and creative way. Being entrepreneurial is part of it, but it's also about noticing opportunities, making connections, and taking action."

Here are two examples of Michal's creativity through public service activism in some of the places she has lived.

The Foster City Library (Foster City, California)

Recognizing the need for a larger library in her community, Michal chaired a three-year effort by Foster City Friends of the Library to convince their city council to build a new facility. She then became actively involved in raising additional funds to help equip it. Michal's roles in the project ranged from catalyst and fundraiser to advocate and organizer.

The Pocket Park (Boulder, Colorado)

Michal heard that there was a plan to add expensive play equipment to a pocket park. Local homeowners were bemoaning the proposed $9,000 cost. Michal pulled from her magazine pile a recent copy of the *Smithsonian* magazine with an article on what children really want from parks. She copied the article for the association in charge of the project and lobbied the leadership. They settled for a large sandbox and some rocks to climb on—a cheaper and more attractive solution.

Endowing adulthood

The Jewish Fund for Justice (JFJ) is a national foundation that funds organizations addressing the causes and consequences of poverty. Their program includes a Youth Endowment Fund (YEF) that gives young people an opportunity to become involved in thoughtful philanthropy. At the time of a young person's Bat or Bar

Mitzvah at age 13, family and friends often establish a fund in that person's name with YEF as a way of accompanying the celebrant's entrance into adulthood. These gifts denote strong support for the individual to make personal commitments to social responsibility. Monetary gifts to the fund can also mark or honor other events, such as a birthday or school graduation.

Once a year, YEF honorees receive a ballot describing groups working with low-income youth that JFJ supports. They are encouraged to select which organizations will receive the interest earned on their individual endowment account. When an honoree turns 21, they designate their fund's principal to go either to JFJ's general fund or its Family Endowment Fund.

A newsletter written by and for YEF honorees keeps kids up to date on what's happening with the groups they've been supporting and tells them how they can get involved in social action and service projects. The newsletter introduces and connects YEF participants to each other, providing them with a forum for their ideas on social justice with peers who share their concerns about helping create a better world.

Sparking an idea

When Marvin and Kathleen Factor retired from careers as trial lawyers they started a business running the Inn on Locust, a twenty-four-room hotel for business travelers in Philadelphia. As an amenity for the clientele they were hoping to attract, they decided to offer a chauffeured courtesy car for trips around town and to and from the airport, using Marvin's lovingly cared-for 1983 Jaguar sedan (with himself as chauffeur). The service is without charge, but they ask guests to make a contribution directly payable to a rotating list of local arts organizations.

The idea emerged as a natural extension of the Factors' longtime enjoyment of the city's arts organizations as well as their conviction that the arts are generally poorly supported. They felt they could expand their own personal contributions to include donations from their out-of-town guests. Marvin's ultimate goal is to influence other, larger, hotels to follow their example, to allow a lot more money to be raised.

Response at the Inn on Locust has been overwhelmingly positive. In the first month they raised $400 for the Philadelphia Ballet. Though they have the option of not disclosing their address, people have been enthusiastic about including their contact information, which gives the recipient organizations a chance to follow up with these donors.

Joining clients in their giving

Eli Walker owns a small financial services firm in Minneapolis. He noticed that many of his firm's clients either don't make charitable gifts or give at a level that is below their capacity and tax advantage. To spark his clients' giving, Eli developed the "We Care Fund." With this fund Eli commits up to 8 percent of his firm's annual pre-tax profit to match his clients' giving to community nonprofits. (The fund matches up to $50 for each new gift a client makes to a nonprofit and for each gift that is $50 more than a previous gift.) At the end of the first year, more than forty clients who participated in the "We Care Fund" match had made nearly 200 new gifts, for a match from the fund of nearly $10,000.

Incentive gifts

Peter Chin decided to give his children, nieces, and nephews incentive gifts to encourage their philanthropic activity. For every hour they volunteered to work with a nonprofit each summer, he contributed double the number of hours, in dollars, to their college fund. For every $25 cash gift they donated or every four hours they volunteered for an organization before they turned twenty-one, he gave each child or young adult $25 to be used for tickets to arts, theater, and music events. By the time they were twenty-one, many of the kids had been to six or eight concerts or plays that they would never have been able to afford to attend otherwise.

Giving collaboratively

Giving collaboratively not only leverages individual dollars and time, it also helps reduce the sense of isolation and fear that can sometimes mark the experience of giving away money. Here are some examples from across the country of collaborative philanthropy.

Birthday Party

As part of celebrating her 50th birthday, the late Phoebe Valentine, a woman with inherited wealth, gave each of ten close friends a check for $5,000 to give away within the year to nonprofits of their choosing. At the end of the year, the ten friends got together with Phoebe to share their experience. All the donors were delighted with the exercise, and Phoebe was pleased that she had multiplied her giving community and expanded her philanthropic reach. The new donors gained empathy for their philanthropist friend as they got a taste of the challenges of making choices in the face of tremendous need. They also noted that the act of giving—even someone else's money—changed the way people related to them (suddenly they were perceived with influence) and changed the way they perceived themselves (they began to want to be more involved in helping nonprofits).

Note: This "Birthday Party" model has been modified or replicated many times. Try giving five friends each $200 or whatever amount you choose, or jointly give away $1,000 with a group of friends on your next big birthday.

Possibility Sundays

In early 1995, Mike and Janet Valder began a tradition they called "Possibility Sundays." First, they invited about 300 people they knew from all different aspects of their lives—politics, church, work, neighborhood—to join them in building a new fund that would not only give money to great projects but would help build caring community among "givers" and "receivers."

The response to their invitation was tremendous; it launched what they named the Arizona Social Change Fund. To minimize administration they arranged it as a donor-advised account with the Arizona Community Foundation. (See Chapter Ten for more on donor-advised funds.)

Contributors are encouraged but not required to give a minimum of $1,000 per year; among the most dedicated participants, however, are those who give far less. Everyone who contributes to the fund is invited to help direct the money. At a recent grantmaking meeting, thirty-six of the contributors met for three hours and decided by consensus on grants to three organizations. Everyone has learned by listening to each other and discerning the overall group's wisdom. In its first year and a half the fund gave away more than $37,500, with an average grant size of $5,000. Their goal is to build up to giving $40,000–$50,000 a year.

On the four months of the year that have five Sundays, the fund sponsors a Possibility Sunday event at the Valders' home. After a catered brunch, there is a welcome, a prayer, and a half-hour celebration of the nonprofits being funded. The grants are awarded, and participants are invited to contribute toward the foundation's future grants to social change organizations in the community. About a hundred people have attended each Possibility Sunday, including at least ten participants from each nonprofit showcased.

The Valders say, "The celebrations feel like 'church after church,' because they give the gathered participants a taste of the grace involved in committed social change work. When people share their deepest goals, it opens hearts. This is new to many of our friends, who had never before connected to social change nonprofits. This fund has become one of the most meaningful projects of our lives."

Directed Abundance

A collaborative giving program called the Flow Fund Circle began in 1991 when a woman with wealth decided to spread some of that money through others and out to the world. She chose twelve people whose world view and life work she respected and whose leadership and perspective she trusted. She gave each of them $20,000 each year for three years to give away. Later, she published a booklet with a sampling of the grants they gave and some of their comments on their own experience of giving. Here are a few of those comments:

> I was surprised by the rarity of this process. In families and in friendships, you give things to each other without expectation of reward. But it's unusual to have that experience outside of intimate relationship. Being part of this was like introducing the characteristic of familial life into the wider world.

> This process has made me very happy. My job has been to discern what the need is and what the impact could be over the long haul. I'm most interested in what seed could be planted and how it will grow over time.

> This was the most innovative, cost-effective way of disbursing funds I've ever experienced. This process completely eliminates the bureaucracy...there's no cost

involved in the administration, so 100 percent of the money gets to the people who are using it. There's an American Indian tradition of "the gift that moves." What I see as the brilliance of this idea is that an American funder can reach people in the most remote areas of the world, through a gift that literally passes from "warm hand to warm hand, warm heart to warm heart." There's an intimate, personal relationship at each step of the process that links us.

Two challenge grants

Eve Stern first became involved in philanthropy in her teens as she participated in a family fund begun by her grandparents. That fund, she explains, helped pioneer the idea of challenge grants. In 1997, Eve learned that Grassroots Leadership, an organization she supported, had received a $50,000 challenge grant from the Z. Smith Reynolds Foundation. Eve decided to help it with a challenge grant of her own: she contributed $1,000 to the organization for every contribution made by a new donor (she prefers the term "ally") under the age of 30, to a maximum of $25,000 a year for two years. This strategy encouraged the organization to reach out to more young donors, which was part of Eve's goal.

Catherine Muther, a graduate of Stanford Business School, worked for a computer networking company in the 1990s. When the company went public, she benefited and decided to make a targeted gift to Stanford to improve the position and number of women faculty at the business school. She committed $100,000 and engaged the CEO of her company, also a graduate of Stanford Business School, as a giving partner. Together, they proposed a gift of more than a million dollars for three specific uses: a Ph.D. fellowship for a woman; grants for junior women faculty; and a professor-level position for a woman. Cate was clear about her objective and the strategy. Focus, partnering, and leverage were key elements of success. She and her donor partner put the issue of gender equity on the table and offered economic incentives for institutional change. Four years later, 15 percent of the faculty at Stanford Business School were women, bettering a 13 percent average for the university as a whole.

An eclectic collection of giving ideas from A to Z

■　　■　　■　　■　　■　　■　　■　　■　　■　　■　　■　　■　　■

Ask friends to join you in volunteering.

Begin a new holiday tradition: With your holiday cards to friends and family, include a list of ten nonprofit organizations; ask each person to choose a group to which you'll make a contribution in their name. Include a response card and self-addressed, stamped return envelope.

Create a giving pool for your family to disburse annually as a joint project.

Designate charities of your choice for birthday or holiday gifts from family and friends.

Elicit public relations and media support to leverage your personal or family foundation gifts as well as an agency's achievements.

Fund (this will take more money)

an unknown playwright or artist.

a chair (or leadership fund) named for a teacher or activist you admire.

your own nonprofit or for-profit enterprise to achieve your own dream.

representatives to attend conferences and meetings on your behalf.

a giving circle and invite diverse friends to join you.

Give

friends checks to donate to others on your birthday.

career or leadership training, such as an experience in Outward Bound or management coaching.

Hire

staff to facilitate your own dreams.

a public relations consultant to develop a media campaign in collaboration with staff for one of your favorite projects.

Inspire grantees by stipulating with your major donations that the organization have employee non-discrimination policies that protect the civil rights of all.

Jump to lead a fundraising campaign.

Keep your highest intentions and passions in sight and align your time and money accordingly.

Lend

your house to an activist, artist, committee, or nonprofit for their use for a retreat.

your expertise to an organization.

Match

your child's volunteer hours with financial contributions to one of their favorite organizations or causes.

funds with other family members to make gifts larger.

gifts of donors to a nonprofit who have never given above a certain level if they exceed that amount.

Network by telling colleagues and friends about groups you support.

Organize a group of friends into a giving group, with each person contributing and jointly developing giving guidelines; periodically select organizations to which the group will donate funds.

Provide an incentive for family members to give 5 percent to 20 percent of their income annually.

Query your peers about their commitments in the nonprofit sector.

Raise money for projects you love from people you respect.

Surf the Web for funding ideas and analysis (see Appendix F, Resources).

Take a child with you to your next volunteer or service activity.

Underwrite or host a party or event for a valued group or leader.

Value your skills as a key influence of peers.

Witness generosity by asking guests to your home to bring canned goods, clothes, or other necessities in lieu of "hostess gifts".

e**X**hibit leadership by giving an early lead gift to an agency's campaign.

Yield more money by taking a mortgage on your house to help a local battered women's shelter buy their home.

Zip through your mail with your giving plan in mind.

Sample letters

■ ■ ■

This appendix contains samples of nine types of letters you may wish to send at some time to nonprofits you're involved with:

Request for financial information

Request to reduce mailings

Request for anonymity

Notification of withdrawal of support

Response to $50,000 request for endowment support

Response to request for lead gift

Notification to accompany donation

Inquiry to make a matching gift

Letter hiring a professional

Request for financial information

LANGSTON F. CALLOWAY
32 Greenup Avenue, #3 • Butte, MT 84569
(406) 465-8934 (phone & fax) • lcalloway@aol.com

Date

Mr. Anthony Farah
Development Director
Western Association for Historic Preservation
1245 E. 17th St., Suite 19
Helena, MT 77401

Dear Mr. Farah,

As a [current or potential] donor to your organization [or, As an interested member of the community in which your organization operates], I would like information about the administrative, program and fundraising expenses of your agency. Would you be kind enough to send me copies of your most recent 990 Forms? I understand that these records are, by law, to be made available to the public upon request. I would appreciate copies of the these documents within the next month so that I can consider the Association for my annual charitable contributions. Thank you so much for your time and attention.

Sincerely,

Langston F. Calloway

cc: Parker G. Forbes, Chair of Finance Committee

Request to reduce mailings

LANGSTON F. CALLOWAY
32 Greenup Avenue, #3 • Butte, MT 84569
(406) 465-8934 (phone & fax) • lcalloway@aol.com

Date

Mr. Zev Mendel, Development Director
Mt. Zion Hospital Foundation
8925 Clarinda Street, Room 234
Los Angeles, CA 90047

Dear Mr. Mendel,

I hope you can help me solve a problem. I am concerned about the amount of mail that I receive from your organization, among others. As an environmentalist, I would like to request the following: I would like to be moved from your regular mailing list to an anonymous donor or "special services" list. If I am contacted only once a year, either through a mailing or with an in-person visit, which may include the mailing of one letter and a copy of your annual report, then I will feel that I am being adequately updated about the foundation's work. If you can fulfill this request, I pledge to send the foundation a minimum of $1,000/year for three years within sixty (60) days of receiving the annual report or the one annual mailing. If after three months I am still receiving regular mailings from the foundation, then I will assume that you are not able to grant my request and I will withdraw my pledge. Thank you very much.

Langston F. Calloway

P. S. Please continue to list me in your donor list by name. If the list is by amount, then simply list me as anonymous, or "a loving former patient."
cc: Barbara Rossman, President, Board of Trustees

Request for anonymity

LANGSTON F. CALLOWAY
32 Greenup Avenue, #3 • Butte, MT 84569
(406) 465-8934 (phone & fax) • lcalloway@aol.com

Date

Ms. Joan C. Chin, Development Director
Asian American Lawyers for the Arts
1736 W. Magnuson Street, Suite 212
Minneapolis, MN 46742

Dear Ms. Chin,

I understand that you have just joined AALA as the new development director. It's a wonderful organization, and one that I enthusiastically support. Although I'm sure you've been briefed about the major donors to the organization, I would just like to make sure that you understand the conditions for my continued support. I am an anonymous donor. What this means for me is that I:

- do not wish to be listed by name in any publications or lists, unless it is under an "anonymous" category
- am happy to receive mailings, but do not want to be solicited by anyone other than you or the executive director
- do not want my donor history printed out and included in any committee meeting or board discussions
- do not want to be called for any reason, including invitations to events, requests to volunteer, except by you or the executive director
- do not want my name discussed with any other staff or board member, or with any other nonprofit director or staff, even in passing.

My anonymity is important to me. I've worked very consciously to create my privacy and I have every expectation that you will respect and help me maintain it. If you would like to talk with me about this further, please don't hesitate. I realize that AALA may not have many anonymous donors who desire this level of detail. So if you have questions, I will do whatever I can to help you fully understand my request and its implications.

Thank you so much for your time.

Sincerely,

Langston F. Calloway

P.S. Please keep this letter permanently in your file.

Notification of withdrawal of support

SAMANTHA ELDRIDGE
17487 Elder Drive • Chattanooga, TN 37403
(421) 465-8934 (phone & fax) • samel@earthlink.net

Date

Mr. Andrew W. Vaughn
Development Director
The Martin and Lila Harrison Trust
245 E. 72nd Street, Suite 547
New York, New York 10021

Dear Mr. Vaughn,

I have been a donor to the Trust for the last six years. And while I greatly value the important work you do, the priorities for my giving have changed and I feel that a seven-year commitment is the maximum that I want to make to most organizations. As a result, the enclosed contribution of $ _____ will be my last to the Trust. During the next six months, I will be happy to work with you to identify and solicit a donor who can replace my gift. Please give me a call or write me in February so we can talk about this in more detail.

Sincerely,

Samantha Eldridge

cc: Khiem Thi Truong, Executive Director

Response to $50,000 request for endowment support

SAMANTHA ELDRIDGE
17487 Elder Drive • Chattanooga, TN 37403
(421) 465-8934 (phone & fax) • samel@earthlink.net

Date

Ms. Cristina O'Donnell, Executive Director
The Ligeti Foundation
5396 Forest Avenue, Suite 23
Pittsburgh, PA 19403

Dear Ms. O'Donnell,

After many years of supporting your organization, I was recently asked to contribute to the Ligeti Foundation's endowment. In order to help me make a decision, I need to more fully understand your interest in establishing an endowment and I have some specific questions I would appreciate your answering.

• Does the foundation have a cash reserve fund of at least three months of its annual budget so that income from this endowment would not be used for operating expenses?
• For what activities do you plan to use income from the endowment?
• Do you have an investment committee that includes programmatic experts as well as financial people? people who are clear about socially responsible investments that are in alignment with the foundation's mission and programs?
• May I have a list of the members of both your board and your investment committee and a copy of the foundation's investment policies and current holdings?

Once I receive the above information, I will give the request for endowment support serious consideration. In the event that I do make the $50,000 gift, a condition of that gift will be that I receive a regular copy of the board minutes, including the financial reports.

Thank you so much for your time and attention.

Sincerely,

Samantha Eldridge

Response to request for lead gift

SAMANTHA ELDRIDGE
17487 Elder Drive • Chattanooga, TN 37403
(421) 465-8934 (phone & fax) • samel@earthlink.net

Date

Mr. Robert C. Dover, Executive Director
The Brady School
5396 Forest Avenue, Suite 23
Pittsburgh, PA 19403

Dear Mr. Dover,

I am writing in response to your inquiry last month into the possibility of my making a lead gift to the Brady School's "Millennium Campaign." Let me say first how honored I am to have been asked and how initially overwhelming it was to be asked to give ten times as much as I have ever given to the school. But upon reflection, I realize that if change is really going to occur, then creating and maintaining a pool of money for scholarships and to support faculty creativity is absolutely vital. So thank you for asking me. Here are some questions to which I would like your response before I send back my pledge form:

1. I would like to make a lead gift, but not be specifically public about it. It would come from the family foundation. Would that work for you?
2. How could I/we structure my gift so that it leverages more large donations? For example, could we make it a gift that is contingent on the campaign receiving three other gifts at $250,000 or above?
3. I am not so interested in getting tied up with the public factor of this gift as I am in the gift serving as a catalyst to others. Do you need me to put in writing why I feel so strongly about the needs for the school's growth?

I would be happy to meet privately with other donors who may be willing to consider gifts of $250,000 or more, but just don't need the public acknowledgment.

Thank you.

Samantha Eldridge

P. S. I want to be sure that my campaign gift goes to provide scholarships for minority students and money for staff. I will add this to my pledge form; this is really important to me and to the future of the school. I also want to be sure that my gift is invested in socially responsible instruments, so please send me a copy of the school's investment policies.

Notification to accompany donation

ALISON GOLDBERG
310 West Frances Street
Boston, MA 02110

Date

Aneira Puttaswamy
The Attic Program for Youth
483 North 6th Street
Wilmington, NC 28401

Dear Aneira:

In support of the work of The Attic Program for Youth, I have enclosed a $10,000 contribution to be directed towards general operating expenses. Please send a letter to me at the above address acknowledging this contribution for my taxes.

I have also included a summary of "Engage Philanthropy," which is my personal giving plan. I am trying to give order to my personal giving and use it as an example to encourage other young peoples' giving. If you know of anyone who would benefit from reading my plan and learning why I have chosen to do my personal giving in this way, I would be happy to speak with them.

Hope to talk with you soon.

Best wishes,

Alison Goldberg

Inquiry to make a matching gift

NORMAN YOUNG
182 South Street
Boston, MA 02130

Date

Martha Tai
Campaign to Protect Chinatown
5278 Massachusetts Avenue, #6E
Boston, MA 02111

Dear Ms. Tai,

I am renewing some contributions for this year and have been thinking about strategies to leverage my donations. Would it be helpful to the Campaign to Protect Chinatown if I offered a challenge grant? The organization's work is so important to the community; I would like to see many more individuals supporting it.

I would appreciate an opportunity to discuss this option with you further. I'd be interested in hearing if there are specific fundraising and/or membership goals that the prospect of a matching grant would help you to achieve.

I realize that this kind of gift entails additional work for your office. Please let me know what amount would make a challenge campaign worthwhile for you. My donation will not be contingent on the Campaign raising the full match amount. I also would be willing to sign fundraising letters as well as mail them to some associates of mine.

Sincerely,

Norman Young

Letter hiring a professional

JEANETTE LLOYD AND ERIN GIBSON
4906 South Ellis Avenue
Chicago, IL 60637

Date

Dear Friends and Associates,

We would like to hire someone to provide administrative and program staffing support for our family foundation. Ideally, this would be someone who shares our commitment to furthering social change. We are seeking the following skills and qualities in candidates. If you know of anyone who may meet these qualifications, we'd be happy to send them a job description and contact them further, or they could contact us directly.

The position will be situated at our home office, ten hours per week. The main tasks will be to assist with filing, grants management, phone calls, some site visits, and bookkeeping.

The key skills and experience we seek in a candidate are:

• Excellent organizational skills
• Great written and verbal communication skills
• Experience working with diverse populations in diverse communities
• Broad-based knowledge about community needs and at least x years working within community organizations
• At least 2 years of management experience
• Experience in negotiating contracts and paying vendors

The highest qualities we seek in the person are, integrity, passion for the work of the foundation, a willingness and desire to learn, ability to work independently, and a sense of humor.

We need someone who can be trusted with confidential information, is good at meeting deadlines, and able to handle pressures from people who want to access or influence us personally.

Salary will be based on experience and reviewed in light of capacity to achieve stated goals.

We appreciate your passing information about this job widely to your friends and associates.

Best wishes,

Jeanette Lloyd and Erin Gibson

Breaking barriers to effective giving

In learning any new skill, there are moments of frustration and feelings of ineptitude. The following handful of suggestions for overcoming these barriers and pushing through to the next level of inspired philanthropy summarize many of the key points in the book.

As with any activity—from sticking with an exercise program to learning a new language—things get in the way of our learning or growth, or our early determination gives way to frustrations that can allow us to get off track and never get back. We don't want that to happen with you and your desire to be more effective in your giving, so we present here the major barriers many encounter as they begin to organize their giving, along with some solutions for you to try. Specific organizations and networks referred to can all be found in the Resources, Appendix F.

The three major barriers to effective giving we've identified are

- Informational: Lack of information about organizations and activities you might get involved in

- Emotional: Lack of confidence as a donor, volunteer or activist

- Strategic: Lack of the time, focus or support that would help you push through the other barriers

Informational barriers

How do I find out what organizations do the things I'm interested in supporting? What roles are possible for me to play? Where do different organizations fit into the picture of making social change?

Solutions to informational barriers

Appendix F, Resources, contains a wealth of information about networks and collaborating associations that can lead you to more information about who is doing what in the nonprofit world. In addition, you might

1. Attend issue-oriented conferences or panels. Collaborating organizations such as the Women's Funding Network, the Children's Defense Fund, the American Association of Retired Persons, and the NAACP all have annual conferences at which you can learn more about the status of issues, strategies, and solutions. Look in the newspaper for national or regional conferences, issue-oriented alumnae gatherings, or briefings that may be coming to your area.

2. Read the annual reports distributed by community foundations, United Way, alternative federations, private foundations, and the community groups these organizations fund or that you read about in the newspaper or hear about from friends. You may get annual reports or lists of grantees by calling agencies or foundations directly and requesting them or by visiting the library or Foundation Center in your region.

3. Subscribe to and read publications that cover news in the nonprofit world, such as *The Nonprofit Times* or *The Chronicle of Philanthropy*.

4. Attend the issue briefings or workshops periodically offered by nonprofit training and research organizations and funders' associations, such as the National Network of Grantmakers, or affinity groups of givers, such as Native Americans in Philanthropy. The Council on Foundations (see Resources) can refer you to specific member affinity groups.

5. Attend fundraising events to become familiar with the people who work and volunteer for an organization and to learn more about the community they represent.

6. Ask friends, family, and colleagues which organizations they support.

7. Volunteer for different organizations. You can agree to volunteer for an organization for short or longer commitments. Be honest with the organization that you're seeking to find out more about them by helping them for a few hours a week over an agreed-upon number of months.

8. If you're a donor who is considering giving away more than $5,000 a year and would like the benefit of meeting with other donors to consider issues or strategies, or if you would like to consider the power of collective giving, you might want to join a donor network. Regional associations of grantmakers (RAGS) also have periodic programs for major donors giving $5,000 or more. In the 1990s, a multi-million-dollar initiative called New Ventures in Philanthropy created many new donor education programs across the United States to promote and expand giving. The Council on Foundations and educational organizations such as Resourceful Women, The Philanthropic Initiative, Resource Generation, the Third Wave Foundation, Changemakers, and the Council on Foundation's Family Foundation program (all listed in Resources) have meetings for major and family donors who give significant amounts. Call organizations that sponsor donor forums and ask them for their criteria for attendance and a copy of their publication list and meeting descriptions.

9. Write, call, or visit (call first) executive directors or development directors of organizations you care about and ask what's needed, how you might help, or what they perceive is a core or strategic funding or volunteer need. Most often agencies need operating income (to pay salaries, rent, lights, phone, and printing) before they need money to launch a new program. Foundations historically have preferred to fund programs instead of operating expenses, so your support of the "annual fund" or core operating expenses not covered by grants really means a lot to groups.

Emotional barriers

What exactly is my role as a donor, volunteer, or activist? What skills do I need to have or should I learn to fulfill this role? How can I become more comfortable with the idea of giving away what is for me large amounts of money? How can I decide what is an appropriate amount to give?

Solutions to emotional barriers

1. Call More than Money or Resourceful Women for referrals to money therapists or family facilitators.

2. Ask friends if they know of anyone who would be a good "money mentor" or teacher.

3. Conduct informational interviews with other donors who are nonprofit leaders to learn how they organize and manage their active lives. Some questions to ask: How do you manage the organizing aspects of being a donor, such as what materials to keep on an organization's needs, budgets, and contact you've had with them? What personal issues about money, influence, and power have come up for you as a donor or fundraiser, and how do you handle the innate inequities in philanthropy between giver and fundraiser? What has helped you stay hopeful amidst the enormous task of addressing community imbalances?

Strategic barriers

How can I limit my involvement in things I'm not really that passionate about? How can I feel less isolated about how I am planning and doing my giving?

Solutions to strategic barriers

1. Review the values you identified in Exercise 2.3 in Chapter Two. If your current activities are not connected to your top values or priorities, decide

whether you want to graciously extricate yourself from them and seek activities more in line with your priorities.

2. Consider limiting your time commitments. Experiment with allocating a specific time commitment—for example one day a week, month, or year—to your vocation or avocation as a donor or donor activist.

3. Practice refraining from responding to every funding request on the spot. When you receive requests in person, let people know that you'll give the request careful consideration in light of your priorities. When you receive requests in the mail, consider them in light of all the other requests you've received in a given time period and in relation to your giving plan.

4. Join a donor network (see #8 under Informational Barriers). If you want to work in community there are lots of networks from which to choose. It can be fantastic to have a dream, create an initiative, and have other donors or activists join you. For some, it's too complicated a process. For others, it's a way to assure accountability, fun, and others' involvement. See Chapter Eight for some examples of collaborative funding projects.

5. Be attuned to and reflect on the working style that is most comfortable for you. Some people prefer to work alone, while others feel they get better and more diverse information by connecting with others. Some donors love to create collaborative projects, others prefer to work anonymously.

6. Some donors really do have a mission statement, a personal action plan, a budget, and are clear about their priorities. Most are not so thoroughly organized. There are pluses and minuses to even the best of plans. After all that we have said about creating a mission statement and a giving plan, we do recognize and honor those donors who don't want to be as organized or analytical as we propose. Whatever your style, claim it as yours while being open to what others are trying.

Loans to friends

■   ■   ■

What would you do if you heard that someone who had been a close friend in high school had been diagnosed with cancer, was a single mom, and was down and out?

Here are some responses we've heard:

- Do nothing. If she called me to ask for help, then I could consider responding, but it would depend on whether it was a current relationship for me. No need to rescue when not invited to do so.

- I would immediately send her, anonymously, $5,000. No questions asked.

- I might check around and ask more about her situation from those who were more recently close to her, call her, talk and get information about what she said she needed, and then consider based on all that what to do. If she needed financial support, I might ask her about her options, and failing any, give some money but, better yet, I might organize a letter to our high school class and ask everyone to chip in.

- I would go check out what she needed. Often hands-on stuff, like helping with the kids, or phone calls, or bureaucratic red tape (like filling out all those terrible insurance and hospital forms) is just as helpful as sending a check and I'd be more comfortable supporting these kinds of things.

Being a giver presents new opportunities for both connection with others and isolation, for opening your heart and mind to the inequities around you, or numbing your sense of compassion with guilt for having too much and fear of being exploited. You can help make real change that is meaningful to you and others, that respects your sense of self as well as that of others, or you can become entangled in other people's problems, violating your own boundaries as well as theirs, and ultimately being effective for no one. Establishing your own boundaries, knowing your financial capacities, setting your goals, and developing your own budget or decision-making process before you're confronted with difficult decisions—all these steps help.

- I have one category in my budget, called "life's dilemmas" and another called "donor's whim." These give me permission to engage in real life's happenings, but also give me some boundaries for my own protection and self-respect.

- I feel a responsibility to learn to lend money to friends and nonprofits. The banks don't make lending decisions justly. I see it as part of my responsibility as a monied person, and I've come to enjoy it. Lots of people have been helped and 98 percent of the loans have been trouble-free, and have even deepened my trust with my friends.

- I had the best of intentions when I loaned my friends money but in almost every case something went wrong. I can now see my own part in not sitting down and talking about expectations, about mutual goals for the loans, about possible consequences, and asking my friends how we might jointly handle communication and problem solving if they were not able to pay back the loans on time. I just wasn't ready to do all the negotiating and partnership required. I still feel that loaning money to people who need it is key, but I've decided to lend it to community loan funds to eliminate some of the personal complexities. (See Resources for more information on community development loan funds and microenterprise development funds.)

If you're going to make a loan, recognize that it is a business transaction and will be most successful if handled in a friendly but businesslike manner, which means written agreements about payback schedules and interest, if any. If this is uncomfortable for you, you might rather just give an outright gift. If you're decidedly opposed to giving loans, be sure you have a global statement that lets people know that. Saying, "I'm sorry, I make it a policy not to loan money to friends," assures the person asking that this is not a personal rejection.

When considering a loan to a friend, the first several questions presented in the Loan Analysis Worksheet for use with loans to organizations (see Worksheet 9.1) will be helpful.

In addition, there are some emotional aspects to loaning money to friends that may not be present in loans to organizations. You might consider the following emotional features that come into play. Place an X at the point along each continuum you feel would best represent the impact of the transaction.

Questions concerning loans to friends

I

am happy to help   feel obligated

Our relationship will be

strengthened   weakened

I will feel I am

affirming   rescuing

I will feel

comfortable   ambivalent

I will feel

useful   used

Resources

■ ■ ■

This section contains a sampling of organizations, Web sites, and publications that can help you pursue aspects of giving that have inspired you to further research. Where the source might not be easily found, contact information is provided.

Creating a giving plan
Books and other publications

Dass, R. and Gorman, P. *How Can I Help? Stories and Reflections on Service.* New York: Knopf, 1985.

Hamilton, Charles H., ed. *Living the Legacy,* (journal). National Center for Family Philanthropy, 2001. Phone: 202/293-3424; Web: www.ncfp.org.

Paprocki, S. "The Why and How of Personal Giving Plans." *Grassroots Fundraising Journal,* 1986, 5(4,5). 3781 Broadway, Oakland, CA 94611. Phone: 510/596-8160 or 800/458-8588; Web: www.grassrootsfundraising.org.

Effective and strategic giving
Books and other publications

A Plan of One's Own: A Woman's Guide to Philanthropy. Forum of Regional Association of Grantmakers. 2002. 1828 L Street NW., Suite 300. Washington, D.C. 20036. Phone: 202/467-0383.

American Association of Fund Raising Counsel Trust for Philanthropy. *Giving USA* (Annual). Indianapolis: American Association of Fund Raising Counsel. 10293 N. Meridian Street, Suite 175, Indianapolis, IN 46290. Phone: 800/462-2372 or 317/816-1613; E-mail: info@aafrc.org.

Barber, J. "Family Philanthropy," *Family Money: A commentary on the Unspoken Issues Related to Wealth,* Winter 1996. JGB Associates, JGB Associates, 2405 Pacific Avenue, San Francisco, CA 94115. Phone: 415/673-0689; E-mail: judgb@aol.com.

Clohesy, S. and Reis, T. "e-Philanthropy v.2001: From Entrepreneurial Adventure to an Online Community." Web: www.actknowledgeworks.net/ephil/2001.

Clotfelter, C. and Ehrlich, T. (eds.). *Philanthropy and the Nonprofit Sector in a Changing America.* Indianapolis: Indiana University Press, 1999.

Collins, C. and Rogers, P. *Robin Hood Was Right. A Guide to Giving Your Money for Social Change.* New York: Norton, 2000.

Covington, S. *Moving A Public Policy Agenda: The Strategic Philanthropy of Conservative Foundations.* Washington, D.C.: National Committee for Responsive Philanthropy, 1997.

Cultures of Caring: Philanthropy in Diverse American Communities. Council on Foundations, 2000. 1828 L Street, NW, Suite 300, Washington, D.C. 20036-5160. Phone: 202/466-6512. (available free and downloadable from www.cof.org/culturescaring/index.htm)

Daloz, L. *Can Generosity Be Taught?* Indianapolis: Indiana University Center on Philanthropy, 1998.

Du Bois, P. and Moore-Lappé, F. *The Quickening of America: Rebuilding Our Nation, Remaking Lives.* San Francisco: Jossey-Bass, 1994.

Duran, L. "The Public Face of American Giving." *Grassroots Fundraising Journal,* 2001, 20(5). 3781 Broadway, Oakland, CA 94611. Phone: 510/596-8160 or 800/458-8588; Web: www.grassrootsfundraising.org.

Edie, John A. and Jane C. Nober. *Beyond Our Borders: A Guide to Making Grants Outside the United States.* The Council on Family Foundation Library Series (a set of four books on family issues, governance, grantmaking, and management). The Council on Foundations, 1997. 1828 L Street, NW, Suite 300, Washington, D.C. 20036-5160. Phone: 202/466-6512.

Elgin, D., Gary, T., and Shane, E. Transformation Philanthropy report. Download from www.changemakers.org/donoprograms.htm.

Esposito, V. *Family Foundation Library.* Washington D.C.: Council on Foundations, 1997.

Foundations, 1999. 1828 L Street, NW, Suite 300, Washington, D.C. 20036-5160. Phone: 202/466-6512.

Furnari, E., Mollner, C., Odendahl, T., and Shaw, A. *Exemplary Grantmaking Practices Manual.* San Diego: National Network of Grantmakers, 1997. 1717 Kettner Boulevard, Suite 110, San Diego, CA 92101. Phone: 619/231-1348; E-mail: nng@nng.org.

Grace, K. S. and Wendroff, A. L. *High Impact Philanthropy: How Donors, Boards and Nonprofit Organizations Can Transform Communities.* New York: John Wiley & Sons, 2000.

Graham, R. *Fifty/Fifty at Fifty.* Carmel, CA: Pacific Rim Publishers, 1997. P.O. Box 1776, Carmel, CA, 93921. Phone: 888/361-4667.

Hall-Russell, C. and Kasberg, R. *African American Tradition of Giving and Serving: A Midwest Perspective.* Indianapolis: Indiana University Center on Philanthropy, 1997.

Hollender, J. *How to Make the World a Better Place: A Guide to Doing Good.* New York: Norton, 1995.

Hyde, L. *The Gift: Imagination and the Erotic Life of Property.* New York: Vintage, 1983.

INDEPENDENT SECTOR. *Materials for Today's Leaders in Voluntary Action.* Washington, D.C.: INDEPENDENT SECTOR.. 1200 18th Street, NW, Suite 200, Washington, D.C. 20036. Phone: 202/467-6100; Web: www.indepsec.org.

Lawson, D. M. *Give to Live: How Giving Can Change Your Life.* Poway, CA: ALTI, 1991.

Lawson, D. M. *Volunteering.* Poway, CA: ALTI, 1998.

Levy, J. *Is it Better to Give than to Receive?* Free from 842 Autumn Lane, Mill Valley, CA 94941. Phone: 415/383-3951; E-mail: levy842al@aol.com.

Livingston, R. and Livingston, L. *Smart and Caring: A Donor's Guide to Major Gifting.* Boston: The Council on Foundations, 1999. 1828 L Street, NW, Suite 300, Washington, D.C. 20036-5160. Phone: 202/466-6512.

Mogil, C. and Slepian, A. *We Gave Away a Fortune.* Philadelphia: New Society Publishers, 1993.

More Than Money. *Welcome to Philanthropy: Resources for Individuals and Families Exploring Social Change Giving.* Arlington, MA: More Than Money, 2000. P.O. Box 1094. Arlington, MA 02474-1084.

Odendahl, T. *Charity Begins at Home: Generosity & Self-Interest Among the Philanthropic Elite.* New York: Basic Books, 1990.

Ostrander, S. A. *Money for Change: Social Movement Philanthropy at the Haymarket People's Fund.* Philadelphia: Temple University Press, 1995.

Price, S. C. *The Giving Family.* Washington, D.C.: Council on Foundations, 2001. 1828 L Street NW, Suite 300, Washington D.C. 20036. Phone: 202/466-6512

Rosenberg, C. Jr. *Wealthy and Wise: How You and America Can Get the Most of Your Giving.* Boston: Little, Brown, 1994.

Schervish, P. *Taking Giving Seriously.* Indianapolis: Indiana University Center on Philanthropy, 1993.

Shaw, A. *Preserving the Public Trust: A Study of Exemplary Practices in Grantmaking.* San Diego: National Network of Grantmakers, 1997. 1717 Kettner Boulevard, Suite 110, San Diego, CA 92101. Phone: 619/231-1348; Web: www.nng.org.

Shaw, S. C. and Taylor, M. A. *Reinventing Fundraising: Realizing the Potential of Women's Philanthropy.* San Francisco: Jossey Bass, 1995.

Shaw-Hardy, S. *Creating a Women's Giving Circle.* Madison: Women's Philanthropy Institute, 2000.

Something Ventured: An Innovative Model in Philanthropy. Washington Women's Foundation, 2002. 1325 Fourth Avenue, Suite 1200, Seattle, WA 98101. Phone: 206/340-1710.

Vaughan, G. For-Giving: A Feminist Criticism of *Exchange.* Austin: Plain View Press, 1997. P.O. Box 33311, Austin, TX 78764. Phone: 512/441-2452; Web: www.plainviewpress.com.

Wells, R. A. *The Honor of Giving: Philanthropy in Native America.* Indianapolis: Indiana University Center on Philanthropy, 1998.

"What Makes Giving Satisfying?" (Issue #2), "Creative Giving: Stepping Beyond the Norm" (Issue #12), and "Family Foundations" (Issue #16). *More Than Money.* P.O. Box 1094. Arlington, MA 02474-1084. Phone: 877/648-0776; Web: www.morethanmoney.org.

Why Fund Media: Stories from the Field, The Council on Foundations, 2002. 1828 L Street, NW, Suite 300, Washington, D.C. 20036-5160. 202/466-6512.

Newsletters and magazines

The Chronicle of Philanthropy. The bi-weekly newspaper of the nonprofit sector. Phone: 800/842-7817; Web: www.philanthropy.com.

Foundation News and Comments. The monthly magazine of the Council on Foundations. Phone: 800/771-8187; Web: www.foundationnews.org.

Initiatives: A Newsletter on Strategic Philanthropy. The Philanthropic Initiative. 77 Franklin Street, Boston, MA 02110. Phone: 617/338-2590; E-mail: get2us@tpi.org; Web: www.tpi.org.

More Than Money. A monthly magazine about all issues of having wealth. P.O. Box 1094, Arlington, MA 02474-1094. Phone: 781/648-0776; Web: www.morethanmoney.org.

Responsive Philanthropy. National Committee for Responsive Philanthropy. 2001 S Street, NW, Suite 620, Washington, D.C. 20009. Phone: 202/387-9177; Web: www.ncrp.org.

Too Much, a Quarterly Commentary on Capping Excessive Income and Wealth. Council on International and Public Affairs (CIPA) and United for a Fair Economy. CIPA, 777 United Nations Plaza, Suite 3C, New York, NY 10017. Phone: 212/972-9877.

Women's Philanthropy Institute News. Women's Philanthropy Institute. 134 West University, Suite 105, Rochester, MI 48307. Phone: 248/651-3552; Web: www.women-philanthropy.org

Philanthropic consulting firms

Cambridge Consulting, Cambridge, MA. Phone: 617/864-8020; E-mail: info@cambridgeconsulting.com.

Class Action, 245 Main Street #207, Northampton, MA 01060. Phone: 413/585-9709; E-mail: jladd@igc.org.

Community Consulting Services, Tracy Gary, P.O. Box 428, Ross, CA 94957. Phone: 415/461-5539, 415/377-9447, 713/528-9166. Web: www.massmanassociates.com; E-mail: tracygary1@aol.com.

Draper Consulting Group, 10811 Washington Boulevard Suite 380, Culver City, CA 90232. Phone: 310/559-3424; Fax: 310/559-4586; Web: www.drapergroup.com.

Eye On The Prize: Coaching for Success, 61 Rosemont Avenue, Portland, ME 04103. Phone: 207/772-3246; Fax: 207/772-3297; E-mail: doug@dougmalcolm.com; Web: www.dougmalcolm.com.

Family Philanthropy Resources, San Diego, CA. Phone: 619/295-5088; E-mail: famphilres@aol.com

Grants Management Associates, 77 Summer Street, Suite 800, Boston, MA 02110-1006. Phone: 617/426-7172; Fax: 617/426-5441; E-mail: philanthropy@grantsmanagement.com; Web: www.grantsmanagement.com.

Mickey MacIntyre, 12974 Furnace Mountain Road, Lovettsville, VA 22080. Phone: 540/822-4663; Fax: 540/822-4659; E-mail: mickeym@aol.com.

National Center for Family Philanthropy, 1220 19th Street, NW, Suite 804, Washington, D.C. 20036. Phone: 202/293-3424; Fax: 202/293-3424; Web: www.ncfp.org.

Paul Comstock, Houston, TX. Phone: 713/977-2694; E-mail: plcco@aol.com.

Proteus Fund, 264 N. Pleasant Street Amherst, MA 01002. Phone: 413/256-0349.

The Philanthropic Collaborative, Room 5600, 30 Rockefeller Plaza, New York, NY 10112. Phone: 212/649-5949; Web: www.rockco.com/website/Html/phil003.htm.

The Philanthropic Initiative, 77 Franklin Street, Boston, MA 02110. Phone: 617/338-2590; E-mail: get2us@tpi.org; Web: www.tpi.org.

Philanthropic Strategies, 1730 M Street NW, Suite 204, Washington, D.C. 20036. Phone: 202/338-8055.

Philanthropic Ventures Foundation, Oakland, CA. Phone: 510/645-1890.

Strategic Philanthropy, 1300 W. Belmont Avenue, Chicago, IL 60657-3200, Phone: 773/880-1703.

Strategic Philanthropy, Australia, 165 Flinders Street, Melbourne VIC 3000. Phone: 03/650-4400.

Virginia Hubbell Associates, 283 Second Street East, Sonoma, CA 95476. Phone: 707/938-8248; Fax: 707/939-9311; E-mail: vhubbell@sonic.net.

Wellspring Advisors, 1420 Locust Street, #300, Philadelphia, PA 19102. Phone: 215/731-9642; Fax: 215/731-0643; E-mail: apark@WellspringAdvisors.com

For more philanthropic consultants, see: *Taking Charge: More Than Money Resource Guide,* More Than Money, 2002. P.O. Box 1094, Arlington, MA 02474-1094. Phone: 781/648-0776; Web: www.morethanmoney.org.

Organizations

African American Legacy Program, Community Foundation of Southeastern Michigan An initiative of African-American organizations in partnership with the Community Foundation for Southeastern Michigan that helps individuals develop strategies for personal and family financial planning and advance charitable giving options. 333 West Fort Street, Suite 2010, Detroit, MI 48226. Phone: 313/961-6675; Web: www.cfsem.org.

Association of Fundraising Professionals Offers workshops, professional training, conferences, and publications. 1101 King Street, Suite 700, Alexandria, Virginia 22314-2967. Phone: 800/666-FUND or 703/684-0410; Web: www.afpnet.org.

Association of Small Foundations Provides technical support and administrative resources for foundations that have less than $1 million in assets. 4905 Del Ray Avenue, Suite 308, Bethesda, MD 20814. Phone: 301/907-3337; Web: www.smallfoundations.org.

Council on Foundations Provides substantial national support services for different sectors of philanthropy, including family foundations. Offers conferences, many practical reference publications, and information about philanthropic affinity groups, family foundations, and regional associations of grantmakers. 1828 L Street NW, #300, Washington, D.C. 20036. Phone: 202/466-6512; Web: www.cof.org.

Forum of Regional Associations of Grantmakers Promotes expanded, effective philanthropy by enhancing the capacity of regional associations of grantmakers (RAGs). Provides local leadership to grantmakers on four important issues: regional capacity building, public policy, promoting the growth of new philanthropy, and communications and technology. 1828 L Street, N.W., Suite 300, Washington, D.C. 20036-5168. Phone: 202/467-0383; Web: www.givingforum.org.

Foundation Center Conducts and disseminates research on philanthropy and education and training on the grantseeking process. Provides information and services through Web site, print, and electronic publications. Includes five library and learning centers and a network of collaborating collections. 79 Fifth Avenue, New York, NY 10003-3076. Phone: 212/620-4230 or 800/424-9836; Web: www.fdncenter.org.

The Gill Foundation Outgiving Project Seeks to increase the overall funding base for organizations serving the lesbian, gay, bisexual, and transgendered communities. Offers donors resources to enhance their giving, including conferences for those giving $10,000 or more to gay and lesbian projects. 2215 Market Street, Suite 205, Denver CO. Phone: 303/292-4455; Web: www.gillfoundation.org.

Grantmakers Without Borders A project of the International Donor's Dialogue and the International Working Group of the National Network for Grantmakers. Provides free advice, alternative sources of information, and opportunities for communication among international donors. Facilitates workshops at philanthropic conferences and initiates media and advocacy campaigns. P.O. Box 181282, Boston, MA 02118. Phone: 617/794-2252; Web: www.internationaldonors.org.

Ma'yan Conducts workshops for Jewish women on service and philanthropy. c/o JCC, 15 W. 65th Street, 8th Floor, New York, NY 10023. Phone: 212/580-0099; Web: www.mayan.org.

Ministry of Money Offers programs exploring money, wealth, and meaning from a Christian perspective. Weekend workshops, trips to Third World countries, and a bi-monthly newsletter. 11315 Neelsville Church Road, Germantown, MD 20876. Phone: 301/428-9560; Web: www.ministryofmoney.org.

National Committee on Planned Giving Conducts research, offers publications, professional training, workshops, and conferences. 233 McCrea Street, Suite 400, Indianapolis, IN 46225-1030. Phone: 317/269-6274; Web: www.ncpg.org.

New Tithing Assisting prospective donors, nonprofit organizations, planned giving advisors, fundraisers, and private and corporate foundations with a budgeting perspective that helps people decide how much they can comfortably afford to donate. One Market, Stuart Tower Suite 2105, San Francisco, CA 94105. Phone: 415/274-2765; Web: www.newtithing.org.

The Philanthropy Workshop Offers a ten-month course for individuals or families with significant wealth who are interested in developing strategic plans for their own philanthropy or for their family foundation. c/o Rockefeller Foundation, 420 Fifth Avenue, New York, NY 10018-2702. Phone: 212/852-8483; Web: www.rockfound.org. or on the west coast in northern California: 650/329-1070 ext. 284, www.tpwwest.org.

The Women's Perspective An international organization that invites women to explore the relationship of money, spirituality, service, and philanthropy. 421 Meadow Street, Fairfield, CT 06430. Phone: 203/336-2238; E-mail: rwilli7994@worldnet.att.net

Philanthropic reform

Association of Black Foundation Executives An affinity group of the Council on Foundations that promotes the status of African Americans in philanthropy and addresses issues and problems of grantmaking. 550 West North Street, Suite 301. Indianapolis, IN 46202-3272. Phone: 317/684-8932; Web: www.cof.org/links/index.htm

Business Leaders for Sensible Priorities Business owners and corporate executives who are committed to increasing public investment in the common goods that provide security to Americans: education, health care, the environment, and a secure future for senior citizens.

Changemakers Works in collaboration with others to transform and democratize philanthropy. 1550 Bryant Street, Suite 850, San Francisco, CA 94103. Phone: 415/551-2363; Web: www.changemakersfund.org.

Hispanics in Philanthropy An association of more than 450 U.S. and Latin American grantmakers and nonprofit leaders seeking to promote participation of Latinos in philanthropy and support for Latino communities. Offers conferences, conducts research, disseminates information, provides referrals, and manages special projects. 2606 Dwight Way, Berkeley, CA 94707. Phone: 510/649-1690; Web: www.hiponline.org.

INDEPENDENT SECTOR Promotes philanthropy, volunteerism, and research of the nonprofit sector. 1200 18th Street NW, Suite 200, Washington, D.C. 20036. Phone: 202/467-6100; Web: www.independentsector.org.

Move Our Money Offers information and statistics on U.S. federal budget priorities and opportunities for activism. 1350 Broadway, Suite 2210, New York, NY 10018. Phone: 212/563-9245; Web: www.businessleaders.org.

National Committee for Responsive Philanthropy Seeks through research and advocacy to make mainstream philanthropy more responsive to marginalized communities and progressive causes. 2001 S Street NW, #620, Washington, D.C. 20009. Phone: 202/387-9177; Web: www.ncrp.org.

United for a Fair Economy A national organization drawing public attention to the growth of income and wealth inequality in the United States and to the implications of this inequality for America's democracy, economy, and society. Its project, Responsible Wealth, organizes persons of wealth to speak out for economic fairness. Quarterly newsletter and workshops. 37 Temple Place, 5th Floor, Boston, MA 02111. Phone: 617/423-2148; Web: www.stw.org.

Women and Philanthropy A professional association of grantmakers dedicated to mobilizing the resources of the philanthropic community to achieve equality for women and girls. Newsletter, annual meeting, and research publications on specific topics in philanthropy. 1015 18th Street NW, Suite 202, Washington D.C. 20036. Phone: 202/887-9660; Web: www.womenphil.org.

Social change
Books and publications

The Activist Cookbook: Creative Actions for a Fair Economy. Boston: United for a Fair Economy. 37 Temple Place, 3d Floor, Boston, MA 02111. Phone: 617/423-2148; Web: www.stw.org. 1999.

Anner, J. (ed.). *Beyond Identity Politics: Emerging Social Justice Movements in Communities of Color.* Boston: South End Press, 1996.

Beder, S. *Global Spin: The Corporate Assault on Environmentalism.* New York: Chelsea Green, 1998.

Collins, C. and Yeskel, F. *Economic Apartheid in America: A Primer on Economic Inequality and Insecurity.* New York: The New Press, 2000.

Domhoff, W. *Who Rules America? Power and Politics in the Year 2000.* Mountain View, CA: Mayfield Publishing Company, 1998.

Karliner, J. *The Corporate Planet: Ecology and Politics in the Age of Globalization.* San Francisco: Sierra Club Books, 1997.

Magat, R. *Unlikely Partners: Philanthropic Foundations and the Labor Movement.* Ithaca, NY: Cornell University, 1999.

Rothenberg, P. (ed.). *Race, Class and Gender in the United States.* New York: Street Martin's Press, 1998.

Sklar, H. *Chaos or Community? Seeking Solutions, Not Scapegoats, for Bad Economics.* Boston: South End Press, 1995.

Stout, L. *Bridging the Class Divide…and Other Lessons for Grassroots Organizing.* Boston: Beacon Press, 1996.

Wimsatt, W. U. *No More Prisons.* New York: Soft Skull Press. (Buy at www.activeelement.org or www.nomoreprisons.org.)

Where to give

Organizations

The organizations listed here are public foundations and national and international associations. They can direct you to nonprofit groups to give (or lend) to or to volunteer with, or you can give directly to these groups. These foundations are community-based resources whose staff and volunteer committees assess nonprofit groups and organize funding for them. Their annual reports and newsletters describe groups that receive grants. You can also ask for more comprehensive documents (called dockets) that list and evaluate projects and groups the foundation is interested in.

The Active Element Foundation A national, nonprofit organization that builds relationships among grassroots youth organizers, donors, scholars, and artists through grant making, technical assistance, and hip-hop culture. 532 LaGuardia Place, #510, New York, NY 10012. Phone: 212/283-8272; Fax: 212/694-9573; Web: www.activelement.org.

Asian American Federation of New York A nonprofit umbrella organization of thirty-six health and human service agencies addressing the needs of Asian Americans in metropolitan New York. Articulates Asian-American concerns on policy matters, generates human and financial resources, and strengthens capacity building. 120 Wall Street, 3d Floor, New York, NY 10005. Phone: 212/344-5878; Web: www.aafny.org.

Asian Americans/Pacific Islanders in Philanthropy Dedicated to increasing philanthropic resources to Asian- and Pacific-American communities as well as promoting participation and leadership within philanthropy. Two major initiatives include the New Century Initiative and the Philanthropy and Giving Initiative. 225 Bush Street, Suite 580. San Francisco, CA 94101-4224. Phone: 415/273-2760 x12; Web: www.aapip.org.

Asian Pacific American Community Fund Serves the Asian community in the seven counties of the San Francisco Bay Area by providing donor services and information. The Fund works with more than seventy affiliate agencies, from health care and human services to art and cultural programs. Also conducts research and supports educational projects. 225 Bush Street, Suite 590, San Francisco, CA 94104. Phone: 415/433-6859; Web: www.asianpacificfund.org.

Associated Black Charities Provides funds and technical assistance to more than 270 community-based organizations in Maryland. Also supports the interests of the region's African-American leadership. Program areas include family preservation and community and economic development. 1114 Cathedral Street, Baltimore, MD 21201. Phone: 410/659-0000; Web: www.abc-md.org.

Astraea National Lesbian Action Foundation Provides economic and social support to projects in the United States and internationally that actively work to eliminate those forms of oppression based on race, age, sex, economic exploitation, physical and mental ability, anti-Semitism, and all other factors that affect lesbians, gay men, and all girls and women. 116 East 16th Street, 7th Floor, New York, NY 10003. Phone: 212/529-8021; E-mail: info@astraea.org; Web: www.astraea.org.

A Territory Resource Provides funding and technical assistance to grassroots groups in the northwestern United States. Organizers and donors set funding priorities together, conduct site visits, and discuss which projects to recommend for funding. Programs include managing money conferences, panels and workshops on various social justice issues, wealth affinity groups, and donor-advised accounts. 603 Stewart Street, Suite 1007, Seattle, WA 98101. Phone: 206/624-4081; E-mail: grants@atrfoundation.org; Web: www.atrfoundation.org.

Changemakers A national and international intermediary that grows and strengthens community-based philanthropy and social change and offers donor education through grants and programs. 1550 Bryant Street, Suite 850, San Francisco, CA 94103. Phone: 415/551-2363; E-mail: info@changemakersfund.org; Web: www.changemakersfund.org.

Funders for Lesbian and Gay Issues Advocates for increased support of gay, lesbian, bisexual, and transgendered (LGBT) issues within organized philanthropy. Provides an information center for individual and organizational grantmakers and grantseekers, a national directory of funders who support LGBT projects and programs, a guide for grantmakers, presentations, and local and regional seminars. 116 E. 16th Street, 7th Floor, New York, NY 10003. Phone: 212/475-2930; Web: www.lgbtfunders.org.

Funding Exchange A national network of alternative foundations; supports progressive grassroots organizing locally, nationally, and internationally. Community activists play a central role as decision makers in the grantmaking process. Three national and international grantmaking programs and fifteen local funds operate in twenty-four states. The Funding Exchange network gives $3–$5 million per year to grassroots social justice organizations nationwide. Offers educational programs for people with inherited wealth, donor-advised grantmaking services, and an international working group. 666 Broadway, #500, New York, NY 10012. Phone: 212/529-5300; Web: www.fex.org.

Member Funds of the Funding Exchange

Appalachia Appalachian Community Fund, 107 West Main Street, Knoxville, TN 37902. Phone: 865/523-5783; E-mail: appafund@aol.com.

California (Los Angeles) Liberty Hill, 2121 Cloverfield Boulevard, Suite 113, Santa Monica, CA 90404. Phone: 310/453-3611; Web: www.libertyhill.org.

California (Northern) Vanguard Public Foundation, 383 Rhode Island Street, #301, San Francisco, CA 94103. Phone: 415/487-2111; Web: www.vanguard.org.

California (Santa Barbara) Fund for Santa Barbara, 924 Anacapa Street, Suite 4H, Santa Barbara, CA 93101-2192. Phone: 805/962-9163 or 805/962-9164; Web: www.fundforsantabarbara.org.

Colorado Chinook Fund, 2418 W. 32nd Avenue, Denver, CO 80211. Phone: 303/455-6905; Web: www.chinookfund.org.

Georgia/North Carolina/South Carolina Fund for Southern Communities, 4285 Memorial Drive, Suite G, Decatur, GA 30032. Phone: 404/292-7600; Web: www.fund4south.org.

Hawai'i The People's Fund, 1325 Nuuanu Avenue, Honolulu, HI 96817. Phone: 808/526-2441; Web: www.fex.org/hawaii.

Illinois (Chicago) Crossroads Fund, 3411 West Diversey Avenue, #20, Chicago, IL 60647. Phone: 773/227-7676; Web: www.crossroadsfund.org.

Minneapolis Headwaters Fund, 122 W. Franklin Avenue, Suite 518, Minneapolis, MN 55404. Phone: 612/879-0602; Web: www.headwatersfund.org.

New England Haymarket People's Fund, 42 Seaverns Avenue, Boston, MA 02130. Phone: 617/522-7676; Web: www.haymarket.org.

New York North Star Fund, 305 7th Avenue, Fifth Floor, New York, NY 10001-6008. Phone: 212/620-9110; Web: www.northstarfund.org.

Oregon McKenzie River Gathering Foundation, 2705 East Burnside, Suite 210, Portland, OR 97214. Phone: 503/289-1517. Eugene office: 2833 Williamette Street, P.O. Box 50160, Eugene, OR 97405. Phone: 541/485-2790. Web: www.mrgfoundation.org.

Pennsylvania (greater Philadelphia) and Camden, N.J. Bread and Roses Community Fund, 1500 Walnut Street, #1305, Philadelphia, PA 19102. Phone: 215/731-1107; Web: www.breadrosesfund.org.

Pennsylvania (SW Pennsylvania) Three Rivers Fund, 100 N. Braddock Avenue, #207, Pittsburgh, PA 15208. Phone: 412/243-9250; Web: www.trfn.clpgh.org.

Wisconsin Wisconsin Community Fund, 1202 Williamson Street, Suite D, Madison, WI 53703. Phone: 608/251-6834. Milwaukee office: 1442 North Farwell Avenue, Suite 100, Milwaukee, WI 53202. Phone: 414/225-9965. Web: www.wisconsincommunityfund.org.

The Hispanic Federation A membership organization of Latino health and human services agencies serving Hispanics in the tri-state region. Through grantmaking, advocacy, and technical assistance the federation builds and strengthens community-based organizations working towards immigration services, health care, economic development, job training, AIDS prevention, youth services, leadership development, and housing. 130 Williams Street, 9th Floor, New York, NY 10038. Phone: 212/233-8955; Web: www.hispanicfederation.org.

Jewish Fund For Justice Makes grants to grassroots organizations working to combat poverty and seeks to bring a Jewish presence to interfaith actions for social change. 260 5th Avenue, Suite 701, New York, NY 10001. Phone: 212/213-2113; Web: www.jfjustice.org.

Ms. Foundation For Women Supports the efforts of women and girls to govern their lives and influence the world around them. Directs resources to break down barriers faced by women of color, low-income women, older women, lesbians, and women with disabilities. 120 Wall Street, 33rd Floor, New York, NY 10005; Phone: 212/742-2300; Web: www.ms.foundation.org.

National Alliance for Choice in Giving An association of innovative cooperative fundraising organizations. Provides resources, training, and national support to enhance the ability of local and statewide federations to participate in workplace fundraising campaigns and to provide interested employees and employers with the opportunity to contribute their skills, time, and resources to building a stronger and healthier community. Works with fifty-three federations covering thirty-four states. Can provide information about an alternative federation near you. P.O. Box 4572, Portland, ME 04112-4572; Phone: 207/761-1110; choiceingiving.org.

National Black United Funds Seeks to promote expansion of African-American philanthropy nationwide by obtaining access to employee charitable giving campaigns, conducting training institutes and conferences, and supporting self-help initiatives identified as community priorities. Twenty affiliates, twelve local federations, and a National Black United Federation of Charities with forty-eight affiliates. 40 Clinton Street, Newark, NJ 07102; Phone: 210/643-5122; Web: www.nbuf.org.

National Community Capital Association Represents forty-nine member community development financial institutions (CDFIs) that provide capital, training, and other services for community-based development projects in low-income urban, rural, and reservation-based communities throughout the United States. Offers a range of capacity-building, performance-based financing, and public policy programs. Public Ledger Building, 620 Chestnut Street, Suite 572, Philadelphia, PA 19106. Phone: 215/923-4754; Web: www.communitycapital.org.

National Network of Grantmakers A membership organization of progressive funders: individual donors, trustees, board members, and employees of grantmaking and workplace fundraising programs. Works primarily within organized philanthropy to increase financial and other resources to groups committed to economic and social justice. Publishes *The Grantmakers Directory,* which includes National Network of Grantmakers's Common Grant Application, and organizes a national conference and other forums for working with colleagues to promote a progressive agenda within philanthropy. 1717 Kettner Boulevard, Suite#110, San Diego, CA 92101. Phone: 619/231-1348; Web: www.nng.org.

National Office on Philanthropy and the Black Church Designed to build bridges between organized philanthropic institutions and the African-American church community. Increases the impact of foundation resources and the African-American faith, enhances the quality of life in the African-American community, and revitalizes neighborhoods and the larger community via economic development. c/o Foundation for the Mid South 308 East Pearl Street, 2nd Floor, Jackson, MS 39201. Phone: 601/355-8167; Web: www.fdnmidsouth.org.

Native Americans in Philanthropy An association of individuals who seek to enrich the lives of Native peoples through bridging organized philanthropy and indigenous communities in order to foster understanding and increase effectiveness. Serves as a forum for partnerships among Native Americans, donors, foundations, and other interested philanthropists, and improves understanding about the unique aspects of Native American people and how philanthropy can help Native Americans increase their access to opportunities within the philanthropic community. 325 Cedar Street, Suite 300, Street Paul, MN 55101. Phone: 651/221-4008; Web: www.nativephilanthropy.org.

Peace Development Fund Provides financial assistance, training and technical support to social and environmental justice organizations. Offers programs that assist donors to become more educated and effective and to build collaborative projects between funders and other organizations. Box 1280, Amherst, MA 01004. Phone: 413/256-8306; Web: www.peacefund.org.

RESIST Funds small-budget groups in the United States and internationally that struggle toward a broad vision of social justice while continuing to oppose political and institutional oppression. Newsletter focuses on topics of interest to progressive activists. Publishes the pamphlet, *Finding Funding: A Beginner's Guide to Foundation Research*. 259 Elm Street, Suite 201, Somerville, MA 02144. Phone: 617/623-5110; Web: www.resistinc.org.

San Diego Foundation for Change Provides community organizing funding in the San Diego area for progressive social change in the areas of racial equality, economic justice, civil liberties, and environmental justice. 1717 Kettner Boulevard, Suite 125, San Diego, CA 92101-2532. Phone: 619/235-4647; Web: www.foundations4change.org.

The Shefa Fund Provides expertise, advice, and grantmaking services nationally and internationally to Jewish funders. Links Jewish values and ethics with the use of financial resources for social justice and spiritual innovation. Newsletter, annual report, and several publications include *Jews, Money and Social Responsibility,* which discusses socially responsible shopping, investment, and philanthropy from a progressive Jewish perspective. 8459 Ridge Avenue, Philadelphia, PA 19128. Phone: 215/483-4004; Web: www.shefafund.org.

Third Wave Foundation A national activist philanthropic organization for young women between ages 15–30. Informs, networks, and empowers a generation of young feminist activists through technical assistance, public education campaigns, and grantmaking for young women; run by women and men under the age of thirty-five. Produces a conference and listserve for young people with substantial earned or inherited wealth. 116 E. 16th Street, 7th floor, New York, NY 10003. Phone: 212/388-1898; Web: www.thirdwavefoundation.org.

Tides Foundation Promotes social justice, economic opportunity, a more robust democratic process, and sustainable environmental practices through its grantmaking program. Enables individuals to set up donor-advised funds and provides a range of program and administrative services. The Presidio, P.O. Box 29903, San Francisco, CA 94129. Phone: 415/561-6400; Web: www.tides.org.

Twenty-First Century Foundation Makes grants nationally to support African-American community revitalization, education, and leadership development. Also assists individuals and groups to engage in sustained and strategic charitable giving through donor-advised funds, grantmaking training, networking opportunities, and financial planning information. 666 West End Avenue, Suite 1B, New York, NY 10025. Phone: 212/249-3612; Web: www.21cf.org.

United Latino Fund Enhances the quality of life for Latinos through a concerted effort of voluntary giving, through grantmaking, leadership programs, and strategic initiatives. 315 West 9th Street, Suite 709, Los Angeles, CA 90015. Phone: 213/236-2929; Web: www.unitedlatinofund.org.

United Ways of America Approximately 1,300 community-based United Way organizations raise funds through a single campaign to support local agency service providers in the areas of health and human-care services. 701 N. Fairfax Street, Alexandria, VA 22314-2045. Phone: 703/836-7100; Web: www.unitedway.org.

Women's Funding Network Brings together more than ninety public and private women's foundations and individual donors to promote the development and growth of funds that empower women and girls. Some local women's funds offer conferences for women of varying financial means to increase their financial literacy, including workshops on financial planning, socially responsible investing, funding, and women's economic development. 1375 Sutter Street, Suite 406, San Francisco, CA 94109. Phone: 415/441-0706; Web: www.wfnet.org.

International giving resources

Note: We urge you to go to www.internationalgiving.org for a more complete listing.

American Friends Service Committee A Quaker organization that works to relieve suffering, nurture grassroots development, and promote quiet diplomacy in more than 150 sites across the world. 1501 Cherry Street, Philadelphia, PA 19102. Phone: 215/241-7151, Web: www.afsc.org.

Global Fund for Women Funds grassroots women's groups around the world on issues of leadership, access to education, poverty and economic autonomy, reproductive freedom, the rights of sexual minorities, and the prevention of violence against women. 1375 Sutter Street, Suite 400, San Francisco, CA 94109. Phone: 415/202-7649; E-mail: gfw@globalfundforwomen.org; Web: www.globalfundforwomen.org.

Global Greengrants Fund Strengthens the grassroots environment in developing countries by making small grants to groups striving for environmental sustainability within their own countries. 3546 Pearl Street, Boulder, CO 80301. Phone: 303/939-9866; Web: www.greengrants.org.

Grantmakers Without Borders A project of the International Donor's Dialogue and the International Working Group of the National Network for Grantmakers. Provides free advice, alternative sources of information, and opportunities for communication among international donors. Facilitates workshops at philanthropic conferences and initiates media and advocacy campaigns. P.O. Box 181282, Boston, MA 02118. Phone: 617/794-2252; Web: www.internationaldonors.org.

Grassroots International Supports social change projects initiated and carried out by people in Africa, the Middle East, Asia, Latin America, and the Caribbean. 179 Boylston Street, Boston, MA 02130. Phone: 617/524-1400; Web: www.grassrootsonline.org.

International Development Exchange Provides small-scale assistance to community-led development efforts in Africa, Asia, and Latin America. International Development Exchange links sponsors such as student groups, religious organizations, and individuals in the United States with community projects overseas. Sponsors select the projects they wish to fund and 100 percent of their contributions are sent directly to those communities. 827 Valencia Street, Suite 101, San Francisco, CA 94110-1736. Phone: 415/824-8384; Web: www.idex.org.

Lambi Fund of Haiti Channels financial and material resources to community-based organizations and nationally organized sectors working to promote the social and economic empowerment of the Haitian people. P.O. Box 18955. Washington, D.C. 20036. Phone: 202/833-3713; Web: www.lambifund.org.

Madre A twenty-thousand-member national women's organization that promotes the economic, social, and political development of women. Provides medical and educational support and services to women and children in Central America, the Caribbean, central Africa, the Middle East, Croatia, and the United States. 121 W. 27th Street, #301. New York, NY 10001. Phone: 212/627-0444; Web: www.madre.org.

New Israel Fund A joint effort of Israelis, North Americans, and European Jews. Provides grants and assistance to social change organizations in Israel that safeguard human rights, promote religious tolerance, nurture Jewish–Arab equality and coexistence, advance the status of women, reduce economic gaps, and pursue environmental justice. 1625 K Street, NW Suite 500, Washington, D.C. 20006. Phone: 202/223-3333; Web: www.nif.org.

Oxfam America One of ten autonomous Oxfams around the world. Provides grants and technical support to hundreds of partner organizations in Africa, Asia, Latin America, the Caribbean, and the United States to enable these organizations to grow food, devise health and education programs, protect human rights, and encourage broad public participation. 26 West Street, Boston, MA 02111. Phone: 800/77-OXFAM; Web: www.oxfamamerica.org.

Venture philanthropy

Ashoka A global funding organization that identifies and invests in individual social entrepreneurs. Ashoka Fellows are nominated regionally in the fields of learning and education, environment, health, human rights, civic participation, and economic development. 1700 North Moore Street, Suite 2000, Arlington, VA 22209. Phone: 704/527-8300; E-mail: info@ashoka.org; Web: www.ashoka.org.

Center for Venture Philanthropy A forum for community investors from Silicon Valley and the San Francisco peninsula investing in strategic business plans of nonprofits. Also offer online resources for donors. 2744 Sand Hill Road, Menlo Park, CA 94025. Phone: 650/854-5566; E-mail: inquiry@cvp.pcf.org; Web: www.pcf.org.

Echoing Green Foundation Offers full-time fellowships for emerging social entrepreneurs. Provides seed money and technical support to individuals creating innovative public service projects. 198 Madison Avenue, 8th Floor, New York, NY 10016. Phone: 212/689-1165; E-mail: general@echoinggreen.org; Web: www.echoinggreen.org.

Morino Institute A nonprofit organization exploring the opportunities and risks of the Internet and New Economy. Focus areas include stimulating entrepreneurship, advancing a more effective philanthropy, closing social divides, and understanding the impact of the Internet on society. 11600 Sunrise Valley Drive, Suite 300, Reston, VA 20191. Phone: 703/620-8971; E-mail: feedback@morino.org; Web: www.morino.org.

Share Our Strength Addresses the root causes of poverty and hunger through food assistance programs, growth and nutrition initiatives, economic self sufficiency, community development, and advocacy. Their Community Wealth Ventures project garners resources generated through profitable enterprise to promote social change. 753 15th Street, NW, Suite 640, Washington, D.C. 20005. Phone: 800/969-4767; E-mail: info@strength.org; Web: www.strength.org.

Social Venture Partners Addresses the social and environmental issues in the King County region of Washington state. Offers workshops, information, and resources for the personal development in philanthropy of the Partners. Also models and networks SVPs around the United States and globally. 1601 Second Avenue, Suite 605, Seattle, WA 98101. Phone: 206/374-8757; E-mail: info@svpseattle.org Web: www.svpseattle.org.

Nonprofit rating organizations

The following organizations have information about large, well-established charities. Most grass-roots organizations will not be listed here.

American Institute of Philanthropy Publishes *Charity Rating Guide & Watchdog Report*. Evaluates and grades organizations according to percent of revenues spent on charitable programs, cost to raise $100, and years of available assets. 4905 DelRay Avenue, #300, Bethesda, MD 20814. Phone: 301/913-5200; Web: www.charitywatch.org.

Council of Better Business Bureau's Philanthropic Advisory Service Sets standards for charitable solicitations and collects information on charitable organizations in the United States that solicit nationally. Web page contains an index to their reports, with information on whether a particular organization meets their standards and how to obtain the complete report (free) by regular mail. 4200 Wilson Boulevard, Suite 800, Arlington, VA 22203-1804. Phone: 703/276-0100; Web: www.bbb.org/about/pas.asp.

Guidestar Directory of American Charities A project of the nonprofit, Philanthropic Research, Inc. Guidestar reports on nonprofit organizations, including information on financial ratios and indicators in the areas of program, fundraising, contributions and grants, debt and savings. Has a searchable database of more than 620,000 nonprofit organizations in the United States. 427 Scotland Street, Williamsburg, VA 23185. Phone: 757/229-4631; Web: www.guidestar.org.

Council of Better Business Bureau Wise Giving Alliance Rates organizations according to criteria relating to board governance, organizational purpose, consistency of programs, accurate promotional information, financial support and related activities, use of funds, annual reporting, and accountability. Offers free booklet, *Wise Giving Guide.* 4200 Wilson Boulevard, Suite 800, Arlington, VA 22203-1804. Phone: 703/276-0100; Web: www.give.org/.

Internal Revenue Service Maintains a searchable list of tax-exempt organizations to assist organizations or projects that do not have their own 501(c)(3) status to find tax-exempt fiscal sponsorship. Web: www.irs.ustreas.gov/search/eosearch.html.

On-line giving

www.charitywave.com Free charity-support service of Wave Systems Corporation.

www.donationdepot.com Accepts donations and gifts on behalf of nonprofit organizations.

www.educateamerica.org A nonprofit federation that pre-screens national and international educational charities.

www.egrants.org Member of the Tides Family of Organizations, providing screened and informative giving content.

www.helping.org Partnership between AOL Time Warner and nonprofit partners.

www.justgive.org A nonprofit service that seeks to connect people with charities and causes they care about and to increase overall giving. A gateway to giving, this Web site provides resources, services, and tools to give money, time, or goods.

www.just-tzedakah.org The Web resource for donors to Jewish charities.

www.learningtogive.org Developed by the Council of Michigan Foundations, this site contains curriculum regarding nonprofits and philanthropy for K–12 teachers and parents.

www.networkforgood.com This site allows visitors to learn about 850,000 charities and make on-line contributions.

www.resourcelinking.org Works directly with large manufacturers, retailers, and distributors to handle substantial donations of food, clothing, and building supplies.

www.virtualfoundation.org Presents screened community-improvement projects in the fields of environment, health, and sustainable development for on-line funders.

Internet-based resources

Information and support

The Chronicle of Philanthropy (Web: www.philanthropy.org)   A free, weekly on-line guide from the *Chronicle of Philanthropy*.

CompassPoint Nonprofit Services (Web: www.compasspoint.org)   Web site includes the center's workshop catalogue and access to frequently asked questions on a range of fundraising topics.

Giving Discussion List (E-mail: giving@envirolink.org) To subscribe, send e-mail to listproc@envirolink and write "subscribe giving" in message body. Cliff Lindesman, list owner; E-mail: clandesm@panix.com.

Giving New England (Web: www.givingnewengland.org) A project of Associated Grant Makers and New Ventures in Philanthropy. Provides new and established donors and their advisors with a philanthropic toolkit to help individuals make charitable investments. Includes giving circle starter kits and state initiatives.

The Idea List from Center Network (Web: www.contact.org)   Contains a directory of resources on the Web and links to more than 5,000 nonprofit organizations.

The Internet Nonprofit Center (Web: www.nonprofits.org)   Information for and about nonprofits.

Leave A Legacy (Web: www.leavealegacy.org) Planned giving information and support.

Money

Donor support and activism

African American Philanthropy Initiative Supports capacity building and the development of community leadership funds. Materials include an African-American Giving Toolkit and a bi-weekly philanthropy e-newsletter. A joint project of the Baltimore Giving Project and Associated Black Charities of Maryland. c/o Baltimore Giving Project, Association of Baltimore Area Grantmakers, 2 East Read Street, 8th Floor, Baltimore, MD 21202. Phone: 410/727-1205; Web: www.baltimoregivingproject.org.

Donor Organizers' Network A working group of the National Network of Grantmakers. Aims to serve and expand the number of people and organizations helping individuals with inherited and earned wealth to become partners in progressive social change through increased giving, volunteerism, socially responsible investing, and activism. Offers regional and national conferences, study groups, and other programs that encourage communication, collaboration, and mutual learning among its members. c/o More Than Money, P.O. Box 1094, Arlington, MA 02474-1094. Phone: 781/648-0776; Web: www.nng.org.

Jewish Funders Network Networking and education for foundation trustees and staff and for individual philanthropists giving $20,000 or more to Jewish and other causes. 15 E. 26th Street, Suite 1038, New York, NY 10010. Phone: 212/726-0177; Web: www.jfunders.org.

More Than Money Assists people with financial abundance (inherited or earned) to realize their life goals and engage their money, energy, and talents towards creating a more just, sustainable, and joyful world. Offers workshops, individual money counseling, and literature. Also works to organize the field of donor organizing. Quarterly journal, *More than Money,* explores the meaning of money with personal stories, articles, and humor. P.O. Box 1094. Arlington MA 02474-1084. Phone: 877/648-0776; Web: www.morethanmoney.org.

National Center for Black Philanthropy Promotes increased giving and volunteerism in the African-American community in general and among African-American businesses in particular. Educates the public about the philanthropic contributions of African Americans, strengthens and supports African Americans involved in philanthropy, and strengthens African-American participation in philanthropy. Produces national and regional conferences on Black Philanthropy. 1110 Vermont Avenue, NW Suite 1120, Washington, D.C. 20005. Phone: 202/638-2269; Web: www.ncfbp.org.

Resourceful Women Provides financial and philanthropic education and personal support for women with wealth. Workshops, seminars, and affinity groups address financial literacy, personal development, community activism, and philanthropy. Coordinates the Women Donors Network, a national network of Resourceful Women members who have annual philanthropic budgets of at least $25,000 and a commitment to progressive philanthropy. Members share strategies, experiences, vision, skills and creativity. Presidio Building #1016, P.O. Box 29423, San Francisco, CA 94129. Phone: 415/561-6520; Web: www.rw.org.

Threshold Foundation A membership community of individuals with significant financial resources, a commitment to social change, and an interest in their own emotional, psychological, and spiritual development. Encourages members to discover their most meaningful work and purpose and to engage in the world from that place. Collaborates with and funds national and international organizations and individuals working toward social justice, environmental sustainability, humane economic systems, and peaceful coexistence. P.O. Box 29903 San Francisco, CA 94129-0903. Phone: 415/561-6400; Web: www.thresholdfoundation.org.

Women Donors Network A diverse community of peers committed to positive personal and social change. Promotes the informed philanthropy of women through support, education, and practice in the context of community and progressive values. Provides members with a learning environment that fosters relationships and competence with regard to philanthropy, finance, and the psychology and sociology of wealth. Also dedicated to the practice of thoughtful grantmaking. P.O. Box 29353. San Francisco, CA 94129-0353. Phone: 415/561-6513; E-mail: sherryreson@yahoo.com.

Women's Philanthropy Institute Brings together philanthropists and philanthropy professionals to educate and advance women as major donors for the nonprofit causes of their choosing. Offers seminars, a quarterly newsletter, speaker training, and a national speakers bureau. 134 West University, Suite 105, Rochester, MI 48307. Phone: 248/651-3552; Web: www.women-philanthropy.org.

Organizations and networks serving young donors (ages 15–40)

Active Element Foundation Builds relationships between grassroots youth organizers, donors, professionals, and artists through grantmaking, networking, technical assistance, philanthropic education, and hip-hop culture. 532 LaGuardia Place, #510, New York, NY 10012. Phone: 212/283-8272; Web: www.activelement.org.

Adventure Philanthropy Catalyzes creative philanthropy through "cool rich kids" outreach on college campuses, and "under the radar" philanthropic research services. c/o 532 LaGuardia Place, #510, New York, NY 10012. Phone: 212/283-8272; E-mail: billywimsatt@yahoo.com.

Aegis Donor Circle A group of wealthy people of all ages, but mostly 15–40, who are interested in creating an ongoing coalition, network, and community, and a collective giving process that connects participants beyond the "Making Money Make Change" conference. The mission is to empower participants, create a supportive community, give collectively, and inspire others to transform themselves and their giving. Julie Parker, Phone: 415/776-5557, E-mail: seagullinc@cs.com; Elizabeth King, Phone: 415/455-8373, E-mail: snowden@indra.com; Mark Breimhorst, Phone: 415/642-7441, E-mail: mark@rinconada.org.

Emerging Practitioners in Philanthropy An affinity group meant to provide a forum for professional support and strategy among young people working for social justice through professional philanthropy. A national network with regional chapters developing in New England, New York City, and San Francisco. Rusty Stahl, Phone: 212/573-4766; E-mail: r.stahl@fordfound.org; Alison Goldberg, Phone: 617/225-0614; E-mail: alison@foundationsforchange.org.

Foundations for Change Works to increase the number of young donors and family foundations that give resources to social justice groups through shared decision-making processes linking donors and activists across race and class. Provides training and tools for grantmakers to learn and to educate their peers and families about social change philanthropy. 77 Summer Street, 8th Floor, Boston, MA 02110. Phone: 617/426-7074; Web: www.foundationsforchange.org.

Jewish Funders Network The Younger Funders Working Group offers a safe, supportive, and helpful community in which to explore common issues, including wealth, family relations, and the responsibilities of business and philanthropy, as well as the transition of assets, traditions, concerns, and priorities from generation to generation. 15 E. 26th Street, Suite 918, New York, NY 10010. Phone: 212/726-0177; Web: www.jfunders.org.

Making Money Make Change An annual national retreat organized by and for young people as a collaborative project of co-sponsoring organizations that brings together women and men ages 15–35 to explore wealth issues within the context of progressive social change. Third Wave Foundation, 116 E. 16th Street, 7th Floor, New York, NY 10003. Phone: 212/388-1898; Web: www.thirdwavefoundation.org.

Reciprocity Works to build connections across social divides and with young people of wealth to find ways to bridge the gap that their financial wealth can create between them and other members of their communities. P.O. Box 25244, Raleigh, NC 27611. Phone: 919/832-7406; Web: www.creatingreciprocity.org.

Resource Generation A national alliance of people under thirty-five supporting and challenging each other to effect social change through the use of financial and other resources. Participants share money-related information, build community, and connect new donors to the progressive philanthropic network. Programs include monthly dinners in four cities and co-sponsorship of the national young donor retreat, "Making Money Make Change." 24 Thorndike Street, Cambridge, MA 02141. Phone: 617/225-3939; Web: www.resourcegeneration.org.

Third Wave Foundation The only national activist foundation for young women ages 15–30. Through grantmaking, public education campaigns, and networking programs, informs and empowers a generation of young, feminist activists. Houses the national young donor retreat, "Making Money Make Change." 511 W. 25th Street, New York, NY 10001. Phone: 212/388-1898; Web: www.thirdwavefoundation.org.

Money management

Books and publications

Bamford, J. and others. *The Consumer Reports Money Book: How to Get it, Save it, and Spend it Wisely.* New York: Consumers Union, 1992.

Dominguez, J. and Robin, V. *Your Money or Your Life: Transforming Your Relationships with Money and Achieving Financial Independence.* New York: Viking Press, 1992.

Hewat, T. and Gerber, L. *Money Talks. So Can We: Resources for People in their 20s.* 2nd Edition. Cambridge, MA: Resource Generation. P.O. Box 400336, Cambridge, MA 02140. Phone: 617/441-5567.

INDEPENDENT SECTOR. *How Much Is Really Tax-deductible: A Basic Guide for Donors and Charitable Organizations.* Washington, D.C.: INDEPENDENT SECTOR, 1997. 1200 18th Street, NW, Suite 200, Washington, D.C. 20036. Phone: 202/467-6100 or 888/860-8118; E-mail: info@Windependentsector.org; Web: www.independentsector.org.

Kinder, P., Lydenberg, S. and Domini, A. *Investing for Good: Making Money While Being Socially Responsible.* New York: HarperCollins, 1993.

Kleberg, S. S. *The Stewardship of Private Wealth: Managing Personal and Family Financial Assets.* New York: McGraw-Hill, 1997.

Meeker-Lowry, S. *Invested in the Common Good.* Philadelphia: New Society Press, 1995.

Mogil, C. and Slepian, A. *Taking Charge of Our Money, Our Values and Our Lives: Guide to 350 Publications and Organizations.* Arlington, MA: More Than Money, 226 Massachusetts Avenue, Suite 4, Arlington, MA 02474. Phone: 877/648-0776 or 781/648-0776; E-mail: info@morethanmoney.org; Web: www.morethanmoney.org. 2001.

O'Neill, J. H. *The Golden Ghetto: The Psychology of Affluence.* Milwaukee: The Affluenza Project. 759 N. Milwaukee Street, Suite 419, Milwaukee, WI 53202. Phone: 414/765-1355 or 800/688-6670; E-mail: jcs@affoluenza.com; Web: www.affluenza.com.

Orman, S. *The 9 Steps to Financial Freedom.* New York: Crown, 1997.

Rottenberg, D. *The Inheritors Handbook: A Definitive Guide for Beneficiaries.* Bloomberg Press, 1998. Web: www.bloombergpress.com.

Stanny, B. *Prince Charming Isn't Coming: How Women Get Smart about Money.* New York: Viking, 1997.

Stone, D. and Block, B. *Choosing and Managing Financial Professionals.* San Francisco: Resourceful Women, 1994. Presidio Building #1016, P.O. Box 29423, San Francisco, CA 94129. Phone: 415/561-6520; Web: www.rw.org.

Young, L. *Money Book for Young Adults, Ages 12–17,* and *Money Book for Kids, Ages 6–11.* 3478 Buskirk Avenue, Suite 1031, Pleasant Hill, CA 94523-4344. Phone: 925/934-9676; E-mail: letiaymm@pacbell.net; Web: www.moneylearning.com.

Index

multi-year, 99, 110, 111; resources on, 229; sample family plans, 95–97; sample individual plan, 94, 98; total lifetime giving, 54, 55; worksheet, 90–91; yearly review of, 99, 103–109

Gottesman, S., 21

Grantmakers Without Borders, 83, 235

H

Hardy, S. S., 154

Hewat, T., 184

Holiday cards, 206

Holiday giving, 171

Hooft, M.V., 155

How much to give: and attitude toward money, 48; exercises on, 50, 55; and major practices of giving, 48, 51–52; and tax-deductibility, 53

Hunger Site, 159–160

I

Ideas for giving: common vehicles, 132–133; creative, 199–207

Imagining a better world, 29, 34–35, 37–39

Incentive gifts, 202

Income inequality, 12

Income levels, comparison of U.S., 49

Individual donors: famous, 7; importance of, 9

Individual giving plan, sample of, 94, 98

Informational barriers, 219, 220–221

Inspired philanthropists: description of, 129; stories about becoming, xxxi–xxxiii

Inspired Philanthropy, how to use, xxxiv–xxxvii

Inspired philanthropy: beliefs about, xxxv; Giving Model, 197–198

Inspired Philanthropy Paradigm, xxxi

International giving, 82–83, 243–244

Internet, giving via: description of, 159–160, 161; resources on, 246

Investors, donors as, 161

J

Jewish Fund for Justice, 200–201, 240

K

Karoff, H. P., 112

Kent, P., 188

King, M. L., 99

L

Lam, M., 20

Learning curve, philanthropic, 112–114

Legacy statement, donor, 143–144, 148–149

Lehman, Rob, 193

Leonard, J., 174

Letters between donors and organizations, 190, 209–218

Life insurance, 133

Lifetime giving, total, 54, 55

Loan Analysis Worksheet, 124–126

Loans: to friends, 225–227; to organizations, 122–123

Loh, T., 75

Lowe, T., 184

M

Mail, unwanted, 127, 211

Major donor, defined, 118

Major giving practices, 48, 51–52

Marin Independent Donors (MID), 187

McCarty, O., 8

Mead, M., 28

Methods, giving: common, 132–133; exercise, 133, 134–137; frequently used, 138–147, 150–153; new, 153–167

Million-dollar visioning, 40

Minkin, T., xxxi–xxxiii

Mission statements: examples of, 44–46; writing, 41–43

Mogil, C., 51

Money: beliefs about, 48, 49; and major giving practices, 48, 51–52

Money management resources, 250–251

Motivation behind giving, stories about, 13–15

Mrs. Grossman's, 152

Multi-year giving plan, 99, 110, 111

Muther, C., 205

N

Neibuhr, R., 196

Net worth in the U.S., 53

Networking with donors, 188, 190–192

Newsletters and magazines on philanthropy, 232

Nonprofit board members, 69, 72

Nonprofit rating organizations, 245–246

RESOURCES FOR SOCIAL CHANGE
AVAILABLE FROM JOSSEY-BASS AND CHARDON PRESS

Raise More Money:
The Best of the Grassroots Fundraising Journal
Kim Klein, Stephanie Roth, Editors

"When I want to know the answer to a fundraising question, or a way to motivate and teach others, I go to some of the best fundraisers in the business—whose writing appears in this amazing collection of articles from the *Grassroots Fundraising Journal*."

—Joan Garner, Southern Partners Fund

Whether you are a new or seasoned fundraiser, this collection of the best articles from the *Grassroots Fundraising Journal* will provide you with new inspiration to help bring in more money for your organization. Filled with strategies and guidance, this unprecedented anthology shows you how small nonprofits can raise money from their communities and develop long-term financial stability.
Paperback $28.00 ISBN: 0–7879–6175–2

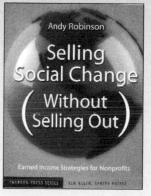

Selling Social Change (Without Selling Out):
Earned Income Strategies for Nonprofits
Andy Robinson

Expert fundraising trainer and consultant Andy Robinson shows you how to initiate and sustain successful earned income ventures that can not only increase your organization's financial security but also advance its mission. Robinson's accessible and lively style guides you through the step-by-step process of organizing a team, selecting a venture, drafting a business plan, finding start-up funding, and successfully marketing goods and services.

Chapters include critical information on the tax implications of earned income and the pros and cons of corporate partnerships and when to consider outsourcing, collaborating with competitors, and securing second-stage financing.
Paperback $25.95 ISBN: 0–7879–6216–3

Fundraising for Social Change (Fourth Edition)
Kim Klein

This classic how-to fundraising text teaches you what you need to know to raise money from individuals. Learn how to set fundraising goals based on realistic budgets; write successful direct mail appeals; produce special events; raise money from major gifts, planned giving, and capital campaigns; and more.
Paperback $35.00 ISBN: 0–7879–6174–4

Grassroots Grants:
An Activists Guide to Proposal Writing
Andy Robinson

Andy Robinson describes just what it takes to win grants, including how grants fit into your complete fundraising program, using your grant proposal as an organizing plan, designing fundable projects, building your proposal piece by piece, and more.
Paperback $25.00 ISBN: 0–7879–6177–9

TO ORDER, CALL (800) 956-7739 OR VISIT US AT
www.josseybass.com/go/chardonpress

Ask and You Shall Receive:
A Fundraising Training Program for Religious Organizations and Projects
Kim Klein

Fundraising expert Kim Klein has trained thousands of groups and individuals to cultivate assets that make good works possible. The *Ask and You Shall Receive* training package is a do-it-yourself, start-to-finish program on jumpstarting fundraising efforts. Realistic time allowances keep the training within reach of busy volunteers.

Paperback $23.00 ISBN: 0–7879–5563–9

(Includes 1 Leader Manual and 1 Workbook)

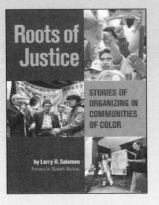

Roots of Justice:
Stories of Organizing in Communities of Color
Larry R. Salomon

Recaptures some of the nearly forgotten histories of communities of color. These are the stories of people who fought back against exploitation and injustice—and won. From the Zoot Suiters who refused to put up with abuse at the hands of the Navy to the women who organized the welfare rights movement of the 1970s, *Roots of Justice* shows how ordinary people have made extraordinary contributions to change society.

Paperback $15.00 ISBN: 0–7879–6178–7

Fundraising for the Long Haul:
New Companion to Fundraising for Social Change
Kim Klein

"An extraordinarily useful book. Kim Klein deserves much of the credit for having defined and developed the field of contemporary grassroots fundraising."
—Fred Goff, president, The DataCenter

In this companion to her classic, *Fundraising for Social Change*, Kim Klein distills her 25 years of experience and wisdom to provide practical guidance for sustaining a long-term commitment to social change for organizations that are understaffed and under-resourced.

Paperback $20.00 ISBN: 0–7879–6173–6

Making Policy, Making Change
How Communities Are Taking Law into Their Own Hands
Makani N. Themba

"A much-needed life jacket for those committed to progressive social change. In a straightforward, full-blast recitation from one who knows, Makani Themba weaves powerful stories of grassroots struggles to shape and construct policy. This book is a requiem for apathy and inaction."
—Clarence Lusane, Assistant Professor, School of International Service, American University

Paperback $19.00 ISBN: 0–7879–6179–5
